301 ways
to Make RV Travel
Safer, Easier, and
More Fun

To Chuck and Cindy,
It's a pleasure to meet
you! Warmest best wishes
as you travel in your
new 40' Motorhome!
Theriece Beard
1/20/2005

PART OF THE

At Your Own Pace

SERIES

ALSO BY BERNICE BEARD

At Your Own Pace:

Traveling Your Way in Your Motorhome

Alaska at Your Own Pace:

Traveling by RV Caravan

Colorado at Your Own Pace:

Traveling by Motorhome with Friends

301 Ways
to Make RV Travel Safer, Easier, and More Fun

Bernice Beard

ARBOR HOUSE PUBLISHING

Westminster, Maryland

FIRST EDITION

Grateful acknowledgment is made to Animalia Publishing for permission to use extended material from copyrighted works. From *Creating a Peaceable Kingdom: How to Live with More Than One Pet* and *Canine Adventures: Fun Things to Do with Your Dog,* by Cynthia Miller, Animalia Publishing, (530) 755-1318, copyright 1997and 1999, reprinted with permission.

Arbor House Publishing
332-140 Village Road, #7-197
Westminster, MD 21157
Tel: (410) 857-4146, (800) 966-4146; Fax: (410) 857-3835
www.detailsplease.com/arborhousepublishing

Ordering Information
Quantity sales. Special discounts are available on quantity purchases by corporations, associations, and others. For details, contact the "Special Sales Department" at the Arbor House Publishing address above.

Printed in the United States of America

Library of Congress Cataloging-in-Publication Data
    Beard, Bernice, 1927–
301 ways to make RV travel safer, easier, and more fun / by Bernice Beard
    1st ed.   p. cm.
    Includes appendix and index.
    International Standard Book Number: 0-9653063-6-4
1. Recreational vehicles–United States   2. Recreational vehicle living   3. Automobile
    travel–United States   4. United States–Description and Travel
796.790973—dc21   2002
Library of Congress Catalog Card Number: 2001117523   CIP First Edition

Editorial services: PeopleSpeak
Jacket design: Sue Malikowski, Autographix
Interior design and composition: Beverly Butterfield, Girl of the West Productions

07 06 05 04 03 02   10 9 8 7 6 5 4 3 2

To Paul,
my favorite RVer

Contents

viii

Acknowledgments

My deep, heartfelt thanks go to the following people: Lib and John Graybeal, for being ideal traveling companions; all of the people who submitted tips, whether or not they made their way into the book; Kathleen, John, Kaitlin, and Kristina Bailey and Fran, Larry, Joe, and Samantha Lathe for their delightful conversations; and the wonderful members of the Westminster Church of the Brethen camping group, for their continued support.

Thanks also to our kind friends and relatives who included us in their precious days as our paths crossed on this journey between the coasts—Elli and Jack Harper; Donna, Paul, Mark, and Elyse Guyer; Ryan, Greg, Jim, Henry, Eldon, and Gary of Dale's Diesel Service; Dave Sprague and Ed Foxmier; Effie and Clem Swagerty; Jackie and Lyle Wrigley; Mary Jo and Bill Cornell; Kim, Linda, and Robert Beard; Irene Cauwels; Jackie and Paul Cauwels; Trudy and Bob Albee; Judy and Fred Martin; Yvonne and Wil Foreman; Vera and Earl Mitchell; Annie and Richard Carroll; Linda and Brian Wentworth and Carla and Billy Fondren; and Lisa, Joel, Tyler, and Emily Graybeal.

I also want to thank Sharon Goldinger of PeopleSpeak and Mary Ellen Gross of Sizzle! for their inspired shepherding of this book; Nancy and Jeff Beard, for their expert graphic art and other contributions; and others who helped in some way but whose names I have unintentionally omitted.

Introduction

IF YOU'RE ONE of the millions of Americans who enjoy traveling in a recreational vehicle (RV), this book will help make your
experiences more carefree.

As I roam around the country, I love talking with other
adventurers who travel by RV. During our conversations, I often
learn about a special trick that saves time or makes life on the
road more relaxing for them. And I'm more than happy to share
my secrets with them—RVers are friendly people, after all. Even
though my husband, Paul, and I have been RVers for 14 years,
whenever I hear someone else's idea, I always think, "That'll
really help us. I wish I'd known that before."

Many of the tips people share have been born from mistakes—sometimes costly ones. For example, when someone tells
me their favorite tip is "Always remember to lower the antenna
before you pull away from a campsite," I picture an antenna that
has hit an overhead obstruction such as a tree limb, is surely
bent, and perhaps was even torn off. I know that the person I'm
talking with either made this mistake or knows someone who
has. By following the advice in this book, however, you'll avoid
making the same mistakes your fellow travelers have made.

I've compiled the best tricks and techniques I've heard from
others over the years, plus lots from our own experience, and
arranged them by categories so you can find the help you may
be looking for. The tips in this book have been tested by experienced RVers and they really work. Among them, you're sure to
find the solution to an RV problem that's driving you crazy,

proven advice that's bound to save you many headaches down the road, and plenty of ways to streamline your RV travels. You might think that a few of these tips sound pretty simple. But sometimes the best ideas are the simple ones—they make you say, "Why didn't I think of that?"

To illustrate how the tips can be applied, I've included a story that actually began in 1993, when 10 couples met in Vancouver, British Columbia, for an RV caravan tour of Alaska. During that trip, strangers became friends. For the fourth reunion of the Alaska caravan group, Paul and I, along with friends John and Lib Graybeal, headed to California at the invitation of Clem and Effie Swagerty. As you read about the trip we made in our new Holiday Rambler Endeavor diesel pusher, you'll see how we took along the comforts of home wherever we went. You'll also see how we handled unexpected problems that occurred along the way.

As an added bonus, the appendix provides details about restaurants, campgrounds, places of interest to visit, the route we took, cost and mileage statistics, publications related to RVing, membership benefit passes, national park passes, recipes, and travel checklists. A glossary with definitions of RVing terms follows the appendix.

The destinations and excitement of traveling in a recreational vehicle are endless. I hope that the tips I've included here help you get the most out of all your future RV adventures.

1

Getting on the Road

NOTHING BEATS the excitement of hitting the road in a recreational vehicle. RVers willingly put in whatever time and effort it takes to prepare for a getaway weekend or long journey into new adventures. To ensure you start the trip relaxed and prepared with everything you need, these tips from experienced travelers will make getting ready quicker and easier.

❑ Keep an RV supply checklist at home. When you're ready to go camping, just pull out the list. It makes it easy to gather supplies, and you won't have to worry about forgetting anything.

—Cinda and Jim Showalter, Mt. Airy, MD

❑ When packing the RV, remember to put lighter items in the upper cabinets and heavy items in the bottom ones. Storing cans or bottles in boxes keeps them from shifting while on the road.

—Mary-Lou and Herb Pletcher (M-LP and HP), Taneytown, MD

❑ Try not to store heavy items, such as large bottles of soda, in the refrigerator door because this stresses the hinges of the door and can possibly cause the door to come open on the road.

—Curtis Greene, Service Manager, Endless Summer RV's, Frederick, MD

❏ Always bring cord and plenty of clothespins for a makeshift clothesline for wet clothes/towels/blankets.

—Lorraine Jones, Westminster, MD

❏ If your trip will take you across state lines, do not take along live plants in your RV because some states do not allow them.

—Bonnie Talbert, New Windsor, MD

❏ Some police/sheriff departments will do vacation checks of your home on request. We use a dawn-to-dusk light mounted on the garage that lights up our place. A lot of people use timers to turn on lights inside at different times so their place looks lived in. Be sure to lock up everything as good as you can before you leave.

—Laurie Peterson, Big Arm, MT

❏ Keep a checklist of things to remember at home before you leave and a checklist of items you'll need at the campground. Planning menus ahead helps. Small containers of personal items can be left in the camper so it isn't necessary to pack them each time.

—M-LP and HP

❏ Stock up on brands that you like at home so you'll have a supply to last the trip. Stores in other areas may not carry your favorite brands, and campground stores usually charge higher prices.

❏ Figure out a budget and then decide how you're going to pay for the trip. Take enough traveler's checks or make sure you have money in your checking account or can transfer funds while you're on the road.

❏ To help ensure that your home isn't an attractive target for burglars when you're away for more than a couple of days, temporarily stop your mail and newspaper delivery. A phone call to your newspaper's customer service number will do, but you probably will have to notify the post office in writing. Pick up an "Authorization to Hold Mail" form (PS Form 8076) from your local post office, or visit the "Forms" page of www.usps.gov. The post office will hold your mail for up to 30 days, so if your trip will be longer than a month, you'll need to make other arrangements, such as forwarding your mail or asking someone to pick it up for you. It's also a good idea to have a neighbor check your doorstep from time to time to clear away any fliers left by solicitors.

❑ Turn on the refrigerator in the RV a day before you begin loading it (two days before in hot weather) to confirm that it is working and sufficiently cool.

❑ Test your RV's gas stove, hot water heater, and furnace. Be sure that your propane tank is filled to the proper amount.

❑ Test the air conditioner and the auxiliary generator to be sure they run properly.

❑ Save steps and time when loading your rig by designating a table or area in your home (a place that is on the way to the RV) for items you want to take along on the trip. As you accumulate items, such as laundered towels for the RV, place them on the table. When you go to the RV, the items are in sight, ready to go along with you. Also put notes there of what you want to remember to bring into the house from the RV.

❑ The day before you take off on your trip, as you go through your daily routines, think about whether you need to take along that medicine or those cosmetics or that cereal. If so, put it in the designated area with items to go to the RV.

❑ Take rain gear and an umbrella even if you think there is no possibility you might need them. The same goes for warm jackets and blankets.

❏ Leave your house clean and orderly. When you return, you'll be glad you did.

❏ Take a road atlas or map of each state in which you plan to travel. Also keep a truck stop directory on hand. You may need to use it to find propane, fuel, or impromptu overnight parking.

❏ Plan a place for maps, tour books, and campground directories within reach of the passenger seat, where the navigator can use them as you travel. For example, stow the items in a compartment above the dashboard on the passenger side or store them just behind the passenger seat in a box.

❏ Leave your cares at home—but take a cellular phone along for emergencies on the road (and so that family members can reach you, if necessary).

❏ Make sure the motorhome is regularly serviced and kept in good mechanical condition. Be prepared with a few critical items, such as
  • extra drive belts for engine accessories
  • a fuel filter
  • spare top and bottom radiator hoses
  • a few feet of extra heater hose
  • electrical wire and crimp-on terminals
  • extra 12-volt fuses for both coach and chassis systems
  • rolls of duct and electrical tape
  • a hydraulic jack with the capacity to lift your rig
  • a few clean rags
  • flares
  • reflective warning signs

❏ Pack a basic tool kit, which should at least include
  • wrenches
  • flat and Phillips head screwdrivers

- socket set
- pliers
- a spark plug socket wrench
- quality jumper cables
- a flashlight with spare batteries
- an inexpensive electric test light or
- voltmeter to diagnose electrical difficulties

❏ If space permits, take along two or three weeks' worth of clothes so you don't have to do laundry very often on a trip. If you're taking young children along, pack about twice as many clothes for them as you do for yourself. Children and messes just seem to go hand in hand. (Note: You'll find lots of additional tips on traveling with children in chapter 17.) Campground laundries are usually well equipped and clean, but it's a lot more fun to be with the rest of the crowd instead of alone in a laundry room.

❏ Take along a reliable alarm clock. Yes, you're on vacation, but you won't want to miss out on special events because you overslept.

❏ Film is usually cheaper at home than on the road. Even if you pack more than you think you'll need, you'll probably still run out.

❏ A portable clothes rack in the house can make packing easier. Hang clothes on the rack as you decide to take them and they'll stay neat until you're ready to hang them in the RV.

❏ If your toddler just can't get to sleep without a favorite toy, blanket, or story tape, by all means don't forget to bring it along with you.

❏ Take a minute for one last trip through the house to reassure yourself that you haven't overlooked something. It's better than worrying later about whether you unplugged the coffee maker or locked the back door.

❏ If you want to get an early start, sleep in your RV the night before your departure so you can pull away without the usual last-minute check of the house. Transfer any breakfast items to the RV in the evening and eliminate the frantic rush—and cleanup—in the morning.

——————— ◇ ———————

Our Journey Begins

IN HIGH SPIRITS, Paul settled into the driver's seat and I into the navigator's (passenger's) seat of the motorhome beside our house in the cool, early sunlight of Tuesday morning, the day after Labor Day. We headed out our driveway to team up with friends John and Lib Graybeal for our fourth caravan together— this time from our homes in Maryland to the West Coast.

During the summer, we had been busy preparing for the trip. In July, the Graybeals and we planned our itinerary. I had previously sent John a list of what Paul and I wanted to do on the trip. When we met, John had a pad of lined yellow paper with his calculations of distances and possible routes. He began with Day 1 and we all made suggestions so that in the end we had a good idea of what the journey would include while also leaving time for impromptu side trips.

Paul and I followed the checklist in the appendix as we prepared for the upcoming motorhome trip. In addition, Paul drove the motorhome to a Freightliner Corporation service center in response to a recall of the vehicle data computer. I worked into the night clearing my desk at home and preparing files and office supplies that I wanted to take along. I wanted to have more experience in driving the new motorhome before heading out, yet I put practicing on the back burner.

I tried to think of tasks that involved some lead time, such as getting clothes cleaned or ordering any products that had to come by mail or parcel service. I unsubscribed from three Internet lists that send information to me weekly by e-mail. I set up in my office an extra card table on which I laid out in order the projects that I wanted to do next. When I brought something new into the office, I decided where it went on the table. The system worked great!

I put office files into a cardboard storage box to be placed in the motorhome on the raised floor of the wardrobe, where it would be easily accessible and adjacent to the motorhome's office space.

As I laundered clothes that I wanted to take on the trip, I either hung them on a clothes rack in the dining room or put them on the dining room table—an area for Paul and an area for me. I aimed to take at least two weeks' worth of clean clothes for each of us so that I would not have to do much laundry en route.

On the day before departure, Paul and I did the final loading of the motorhome. I also ran a couple of errands and got last-minute groceries. Paul completed waxing the top of the motorhome and other tasks—all in great spirits and good humor.

A familiar excited feeling was building inside me as we got closer to leaving. It came from not knowing what was ahead and from the anticipated joy of stepping up into the motorhome, settling into the navigator's seat, and actually pulling out of our driveway and onto the road, knowing that we were headed out to see the world. It put a smile on my face and in my heart.

The first leg of the trip would include visits with family and friends in Ohio, Indiana, and Missouri. For the Missouri visit, I had made reservations at the Osage Beach RV Park for Friday,

Saturday, and Sunday nights during the first week. These were our only prior reservations for we would be traveling after Labor Day, the off-season for many campgrounds. I had to be sure we had a campsite in that particular campground, however, because I had an appointment for a radio interview there on Monday morning.

We paused at the foot of the county road leading past our driveway, then fell in behind John Graybeal as he drove past on State Route (SR) 140 in a Southwind 35 foot motorhome.

John asked Paul on the CB radio, "Milkweed, got your lights on?"

"Affirmative, Chainsaw. Unless I forget, I'll be running with my lights on all the time," Paul responded.

We used channel 13 on the CB and "handles," or CB nicknames, when talking on the radio. On this trip we dubbed Lib "Mall Shopper." My handle was already "Reindeer."

We turned left in Taneytown onto SR 194 and headed to a gasoline station in Walkersville where we caught up with John, who was already refueling. Soon Lib pulled in behind the Southwind in her Honda station wagon. It would serve as the tow car for the trip. John adeptly hooked the car to the rear of his motorhome and climbed behind the steering wheel again. At John's suggestion, Paul took the lead and our two-motorhome caravan officially began.

Shortly before noon, we stopped for lunch at a truck stop at Keyser's Ridge in western Maryland. We dined there in our motorhomes parked side by side. John brought over a box of Lib's fresh brownies with English walnuts. Delicious!

A little more than an hour later, we stopped at the Pennsylvania Welcome Center off Interstate 79 (I-79). By three o'clock we entered West Virginia and took I-470 around Wheeling. In no time, we drove under a large overhead sign in the shape of the state that said "Ohio Welcomes You."

At a rest stop in the late afternoon, John told us that according to the *Trailer Life Directory for Campgrounds, RV Parks & Services,* the campground where we had planned to stay that night had a limit of 35 feet on the length of motorhomes. John's was 35 and ours was 37 feet.

I looked up other campgrounds in Zanesville, Ohio, and found Wolfie's Family Kamping. It had a very good rating and was a Good Sam Park, for which both the Graybeals and we had membership cards that gave a 10 percent discount off the night's stay. Paul and John agreed to try Wolfie's.

West of Zanesville, we left I-70 and wound around on a narrow road through a wooded area until we came upon the beautiful flowers and flag at the entrance to Wolfie's.

That evening after dinner in our motorhomes, I explored the campground. On the hilltop, a gray, wooden, freestanding porch swing beckoned. As I swung back and forth, I looked down at a dirt track with a small grandstand and a small lake with a fountain in the center, both bordered on three sides by wooded slopes of mostly deciduous trees. I heard the purring sounds of someone mowing far off to my left and the splashing of water in the pond. In the cool breeze, a bird called. A half-moon hung in the sunlit evening sky.

On Wednesday morning in cool, fresh air with a slight breeze, we left the chirping birds of Wolfie's, traveled on the good gravel woodland road, and turned onto I-70 toward Columbus, Ohio. At first the gradually ascending and descending highway continued with trees lining parts of it, their leaves showing slight changes from green into yellows and reds. Then it leveled out and we came upon all-too-common road construction. Tree branches moved briskly and the sun cast shadows that danced alongside our vehicles.

We expected to arrive at our next campground in late morning, which was before check-in time for some campgrounds. As a former campground owner, John said that we could let the staff know that we would not be staying longer than 24 hours overall.

When we arrived at the Olive Branch Campground, the office was closed but instructions and diagrams of the campground were handy on the porch. John and Paul looked at them, then walked into the campground area to select our sites. We parked side by side as we had done the previous night.

The following day, Thursday, our two-RV caravan headed south on I-71 to Exit 19, where we met Elli and Jack Harper, congenial friends of the Graybeals, for lunch at a Cracker Barrel near Kings Island, Cincinnati.

Paul and I had met the Harpers once before when the Graybeals and we traveled to Colorado. During lunch, Jack, a former campground owner himself, told us that many campgrounds were providing e-mail and Internet service to campers, some in private rooms and some in a section of the laundry with a table and chairs.

After a delicious lunch and a few photographs, we said a warm good-bye to these special people and headed for the Woods-N-Waters Kampground near Columbus, Indiana.

"I don't get as tired driving this diesel motorhome as the gas one because I don't have to work the steering wheel as much to stay where I need to be—it's more responsive," Paul remarked.

After arriving at the Woods-N-Waters Kampground and hooking up to the utilities, Paul extended our slideout for the first time this trip. With our motorhome, we push an electric switch and hold it in as the slideout section creaks and groans with its heavy load of kitchen counter, cabinets, and long sofa and stops at its extended maximum. When we prepare to go back on the road, we reverse the process after making sure there are no obstacles in the path of the incoming slideout. How relaxing it was to have the extra space in the living room and kitchen areas. Not that we would have much time to relax in it, at least in the next few days.

2

Maintaining Your RV before a Trip and on the Road

REGULAR MAINTENANCE of your RV is the best way to prevent mechanical problems while traveling. The tips in this chapter will help you keep your RV ready to go whenever you want to get away. However, even a well-maintained vehicle can develop problems, so you need to be prepared and know what to do if that happens to you.

❑ Get copies of wiring diagrams from your RV manufacturer and chassis manufacturer. If an electrical problem occurs, service technicians can get you back on the road sooner because they will have the information they need about your RV.
—Henry Ross, Randallstown, MD

❑ Include lighter fluid among your cleaning supplies (some brands come in plastic squirt bottles). It's a handy solvent for road oil, label gum, and grease spots.
—Mary-Lou and Herbert Pletcher, Taneytown, MD

❑ Make sure that you put lubricant on the hinges of your RV's steps at least once a month.
—Shari Williams (SW), Adventureland RV Rentals, LLC, Wichita, KS

❑ Reseal the edges of rubber roofs at least once a year and wash rubber roofs at least four times a year to help maintain their life expectancy.
—SW

❑ Before you travel and at each evening stop, check all external lights as they will sometimes come loose during travel.
—SW

❑ On slideouts that require interior roof props for traveling on the road, tie a piece of brightly colored ribbon to a prop and drape it over the front of the slideout to use as a reminder to remove the props before extending the room. You can damage the slide mechanism or the interior walls if the props are not removed before operating the slideout switch.
—Curtis Greene, Service Manager, Endless Summer RV's,
  Frederick, MD

❑ To clean bugs and insects off your RV with ease, add 1 to 2 teaspoons of baking soda (to adjust the pH—bugs and insects are acidic) to a 10-quart bucket of warm soapy water. Be sure to use a mild dishwashing liquid, not a harsh detergent that might damage the RV's surface.
—Carroll and Joyce Dell, Littlestown, PA, and John Graybeal,
  Hampstead, MD

❑ Know how to get assistance to repair your motorhome and any other equipment that you have with you, such as a car, auxiliary generator, or boat. It's a good idea to purchase an emergency road service policy for your RV. Also, a dealer directory for your brand of RV usually comes with your vehicle.

❑ When you hear a rattle in your rig, check for loose screws, such as those that attach the cover on the range.

❑ Don't overinflate your tires. When you check tire pressure, keep in mind that cold temperatures normally cause tire pressure to drop. The pressure will build up as you drive.

❑ Surprisingly, most truck stops don't carry propane (also called "LP gas"). If you're looking for LP gas while on the road, try a campground that's near the highway.

❑ Use a notebook to record RV maintenance, listing the date and odometer reading along with other details. Set up a separate page for oil changes, oil filter changes, and other maintenance tasks. You may find it convenient to have separate notebooks for some pieces of equipment, like the generator.

❑ A wood tire knocker (available at truck stops) is handy for quickly checking tires to see if they sound solid or might be leaking air.

❑ Most RVers love to talk shop. Be ready to learn from other campers, dealers, and truck drivers. Read all the articles and books you can find and study the manuals that come with your equipment. Then be willing to share what you've experienced.

❑ Pack an old rug or mat to lie on when you need to check under the RV.

❑ After you dump, pour Aqua-Kem Concentrated Liquid Holding Tank Deodorant into the toilet and flush it into the black water tank. This product deodorizes and helps disintegrate the incoming waste and tissue and also helps keep the holding tank clean.

❑ Use a water pressure gauge to check the pressure coming from campground spigots. The regulator on the gauge allows you to set the amount of pressure entering the plumbing system of the RV. Too much pressure can pop loose various connections and cause leaks. To be on the safe side, turn off

the campground water just before you go to bed each
night.

❑ When your engine seems to be gasping for breath, impurities
in the gasoline may have clogged the in-line filter between
the gas tank and the engine. Remove the filter, blow out any
silt and dirt, and replace the filter. A spare filter is handy to
have along.

❑ Your daily maintenance routine on the road should include
cleaning the windshield and checking the oil levels in the
engine and the auxiliary generator. Walk around the RV
to check the tires and look for signs of fluid leaks. Dust off
the headlights and taillights.

❑ Keep in mind that many campgrounds don't allow guests to
change their vehicle's oil at the campsite because of possible
oil spillage on the ground. Try to find an RV supplier with
space for changing oil, or go to a large shopping center
parking lot if necessary.

————— ◇ —————

Breakdown

ON FRIDAY MORNING, Day 4 of our trip, we left Columbus,
Indiana, intending to reach the Osage Beach RV Park, in Osage
Beach, Missouri, later that day.

After passing Vandalia, Indiana, at 10:16 A.M., our yellow
"Check Engine" light came on unexpectedly. When that happens,
a double row of red and yellow messages lights up on the dash of
the motorhome.

Paul immediately pulled off onto the shoulder, telling John that we would catch up with him down the road. He suspected that either he had gotten some dirt-laden fuel at our last fill-up or that the water/fuel separator needed draining—a task he had not done so far on the trip.

He took a plastic cup, crawled underneath the motorhome, and drained some fluid from the water/fuel separator into the cup. Sometimes a batch of bad fuel contains water, which is harmful to diesel engines. Water is heavier than fuel and gathers in the bottom of the separator cup located underneath the vehicle. Paul drained about a cup of liquid, put a paper towel in the cup to blot the liquid, put everything into a plastic grocery bag, and stored it in the lower compartment for later disposal.

Fifteen minutes later we pulled back onto the road. Paul tried to reach John on the CB. No answer. We kept going in hopes of spotting the Graybeals or reaching them on the CB.

Then we heard the faint voice of John. He was sitting on the side of the road in a little town ahead. Soon we heard him clearly and then saw the Southwind and tow car. We passed and he fell in behind us. Paul explained what had happened.

Suddenly, our motorhome gave two hard jerks and the Check Engine light came on again. Paul pulled over to the shoulder and turned off the engine. The Graybeals stopped also.

Paul decided to try driving more slowly in hopes of reaching the welcome center just beyond Terre Haute at the Illinois border, where he could look at the manual and figure out what was happening. He had learned from someone at Freightliner that it was okay to drive after the *yellow* Check Engine light came on. That light indicated that the driver should check into the matter at the earliest convenient location. If a *red* light came on, however, the driver should stop immediately.

About 10 miles from Terre Haute, the engine would not accelerate. We stopped in an empty parking lot for about a half-hour. Paul drained another cup of liquid from the separator and started up the motor again; it ran smoothly.

When we left the lot, Paul asked me to keep an eye on the air pressure gauge and let him know if it went below 100.

A little after noon, we drove into the Illinois Welcome Center between two rows of trucks and RVs. I spotted the Graybeals on our right—a welcome sight! Paul found a pay phone and looked up diesel service in the area. The closest place was Scheid Diesel Service Co. in Effingham, about 60 miles west.

After lunch, we headed for Scheid Diesel. With a hill ahead, the motorhome gave another hard jerk and the engine sputtered. Again, we pulled over to a grassy shoulder with the Graybeals behind.

After Paul drained more liquid, we re-entered the highway. Paul and John stayed in close touch by CB.

We passed an enormous field of soybeans and tasseled corn. Then we felt another hard jerk and pulled to the shoulder again. As Paul searched for clues to our problem, I turned on the cell phone in case we needed to call for assistance. I wanted to call Scheid Diesel but couldn't get through to information to get the number. Paul had only the address. A state trooper stopped behind our two RVs and suggested that we go to a BP station at the next exit and get the phone number from there.

Once more, we returned to I-70. We took the first exit to Martinsville, Illinois, and found the BP station, which, thankfully, had a huge gravel parking lot. It was almost two o'clock on that Friday afternoon.

In his call to Scheid Diesel from a pay phone, Paul learned that the business closed at five o'clock and did not make road calls. It had the filter he thought we needed, but he had to take in the old filter.

"There are so many unknowns that it's difficult to know what to do," Paul told John and me as he got out the grass reed mat from a basement compartment of the motorhome. He shoved it under the filter area, lay on it, and planned how to remove the old filter. He called for paper towels, a container to drain the filter, and pliers to unscrew the plug of the filter.

In due time, he succeeded. I dusted the dirt from his back before he went inside our motorhome to wash the black soot from his arms.

It was 2:40 when John and Paul drove in the tow car to Effingham, leaving Lib and me in our side-by-side motorhomes. I called Osage Beach RV Park to find out how far away it was and if there was any problem with our expected late, late arrival.

I learned that we were still several hours away from Osage Beach. The staffer I spoke with said that she would leave an envelope with our names on it in a box at the office door. We could go to our sites and pay in the morning.

At 4:55 P.M., the men returned from Effingham. While Paul installed the new fuel filter and added fuel oil conditioner, John called a nearby campground for reservations that night. I called Osage Beach again to say that it was too far for us to go that day but to expect us the next day.

After almost four and a half hours at the hospitable BP station in Martinsville, we returned to I-70. Surely our problem was fixed with the new filter installed, but after a few miles the symptoms returned—Check Engine light, jerks, deceleration.

We made it to a campground at Casey, Illinois, and went to dinner in the tow car at Richards Farm Restaurant. Its rustic milieu and excellent food helped us to relax after the day's events. Paul asked at the cashier's desk for the name of a local diesel service dealer. A local resident waiting in line for dinner heard the inquiry and gave Paul the names and phone numbers of three possibilities, one of whom made "house" calls and took calls at his home after normal working hours.

Back at the campground, Paul called that number and arranged for the diesel technician to come to the campground the next morning at 10 o'clock. Paul stayed up late that night reading and studying the Cummins Engine and Freightliner diagrams and printed text, trying to both understand them and figure out what was causing our diesel engine to surge, decelerate, jerk hard, run rough, and make the Check Engine light glow.

Saturday morning, Paul and I stood outside our motorhome waiting for the diesel technician. About 10 o'clock, we watched him drive into the campground in his mobile service truck. A wave of relief went through me. Then almost before I knew it, he drove out again, dust billowing behind his truck. Paul shouted a loud "Hey" to him. I ran to the road waving my arms. I couldn't believe he was leaving without working on our engine.

It turned out that a disagreement between him and the campground owner had caused the technician to turn around and leave. My heart sank!

We called and arranged to meet him at his service center in Effingham, but when we arrived, we learned that he had taken an emergency call that was too far away in northern Illinois for him to help us that afternoon.

Paul called Dale's Diesel Service, another of the places recommended by the man in the restaurant the night before, and spoke with Ryan, the manager, who said he could work us in.

By 2:09 P.M., the Graybeals and we drove into the huge parking area of Dale's Diesel Service at Teutopolis, Illinois. It was heavily populated with semi tractors and trailers.

Paul went into the office and returned a few minutes later with two fuel filters. Ryan was trying to move a unit from inside a bay so that he could get us in to run a diagnostic test on our engine.

At a signal from a technician, Paul drove our motorhome to the other side of the service building and into one of six bays on that side.

Five technicians in uniforms went to work on our unit— Greg, Jim, Henry, Eldon, and Gary. A diagnostic computer on wheels stood waiting nearby. Eldon drained about 10 gallons of fuel, which looked clean without water or debris in it. The oil tank was one-half gallon low, but that should not have caused the trouble we were having.

Then the technicians looked for the connector that would hook up the motorhome to the computer. They spent an hour searching—in basement compartments, underneath the body, and inside the coach around the engine under the bed. Ryan, Paul, John, and I tried to find it too.

Finally, after several phone calls, Greg learned that the connector was in the chassis frame at the side of the engine. From inside the motorhome under the raised bed platform, he hooked it to the computer. The problem: a ground cable loose on the coach battery. That caused the electronic computer module (ECM) to lose power at times. The technicians tightened the nut on the loose cable as well as the other three battery cables and cleaned all of the terminals. One loose nut had caused all that trouble!

Although I was anxious to head toward Osage Beach RV Park, the people at Dale's Diesel Service insisted that we take a test run, and Paul of course agreed.

The motorhome passed its road exam and Paul gladly paid the bill. With the best wishes of the good people at Dale's Diesel Service, the Graybeals and we left their oasis after a productive 3¾-hour hiatus with them. It was 5:44 P.M., light, and still hot as we headed toward St. Louis.

Even though we'd had another delay, we agreed that we would try to reach Osage Beach that evening. We decided to eat on the run as we rode along the highway in our motorhomes. I fed Paul four sandwiches made of chocolate graham crackers slathered with peanut butter and a small can of peaches from a cup. He had a bottle of water at his left arm in a holder on the side panel.

I looked for the famous Gateway Arch during our half-circuit of St. Louis but did not see it. We soon crossed the Missouri River. Since John and Paul had been driving for 2¼ hours, I searched the map for the next rest area.

At the rest area the skies were cloudy and darkening. At Paul's suggestion, I called the Osage Beach RV Park to let the office know our whereabouts and to ask for specific directions. The office was about to close, but the staffer graciously told me how to find the campground. The campground sign would be lighted until 10 o'clock, I was told.

Back on I-70 in the growing darkness, we continued to Exit 148, where we switched to SR 54 south toward Jefferson City. Under the beam from a flashlight, I wrote brief notes in my journal. The three-quarter moon lightened the night sky.

It was well past 10 o'clock when we found our way to what we thought was the entrance to Osage Beach RV Park. It was so dark that we could not be sure. Both RVs parked out of the traffic pattern. I stepped down from the motorhome into a warm night, with flashlight in hand. I hurried up a long incline toward a lighted building. My leg muscles worked hard. My breath came faster. At the hilltop, I walked onto a wide, empty expanse, which I assumed was an RV parking area. The lighted building ahead appeared to be the office of the Osage Beach RV Park.

I turned toward our RVs in the distance below. I moved the beam from the flashlight in a circular motion. I hoped it would be interpreted as a signal to come ahead.

Then I turned and walked onto the office porch. I lifted two envelopes from the mailbox—one marked "Graybeal" and the other "Beard." As I looked at them under the porch light, a man strode around the corner. He was the campground owner. We shook hands as I told him who I was.

By this time, our motorhomes arrived up the hill. The owner and I walked ahead, leading them to our campsites. I looked at my watch: 11:26 P.M. We had finally arrived!

We had been on the road 5¾ hours since leaving Teutopolis and had traveled 323 miles during that day. Our journey could now proceed as planned.

3

All about Campgrounds

THE BEST part about camping in an RV is, of course, being able to take along some creature comforts. "Roughing it" is even easier when you follow the advice of veteran campers and campground owners.

❑ It's always best to make reservations so the campground can plan to accommodate your rig, especially if the area you'll be visiting has a lot of visitors. Also, unless you're familiar with an area, you never know what special events might be going on. The campground you want to stay at may be full of people in town for an event.
—Selena Littman, Candy Hill Campground, Winchester, VA

❑ Make sure that the type of campsite you reserve is what you really want. For example, you might call a campground and say you want a site with electric and sewer service. If you realize on arrival that you really wanted full hookups, the staff may not be able to accommodate you. Also, if you don't stay at a campground where you have made a reservation, don't be surprised if you are charged as a no show. If you can't go to the campground, call to let the staff know, and be sure to get a cancellation number.

Without a cancellation number, credit card companies will
not reverse the charge.

—Paul LeClair, Fort Welikit Family Campground, Black Hawk, SD

❏ If you plan to take your pet on vacation with you, when
you call campgrounds to make reservations, be sure to ask
whether the campground welcomes pets.

—Lt. Col. Virginia Dillon, Alexandria, VA

(Note: You'll find additional tips on traveling with pets in chapter 17.)

❏ To save time starting a fire, bring a bundle of fire-starter
logs and use a small piece to light the fire.

—Pete Jones, Westminster, MD

❏ If possible, choose a level or mounded site. With rain,
a little valley can turn into a huge headache of a pond!

—Lorraine Jones, Westminster, MD

❏ Put something on the gearshift lever to remind you to
lower the antenna before you leave a campsite, or make
a checklist and follow it.

—David Craft, Anderson Campers, Anderson, CA

❏ When draining the holding tanks of an RV, release the
black water first and then the gray water, which helps
clean out the system.

—Richard Hayden, Leonardtown, MD

❏ Traveling to many different campgrounds and needing
sanitary hoses of long lengths has sometimes been a
problem. I carry both a 10-foot and a 20-foot sanitary hose.
I glued a female connector to the 90-degree elbow red
connector that has the screw-in adapter for campground
pipes so I can connect it to either the short or long hose.
Both hoses have male and female connectors on opposite
ends so they can be used as extensions.

—Howard L. Wright, Havre de Grace, MD

❏ Before you leave a campsite, walk around the motorhome to check for connected or items left behind.

—Pete Jones, Westminster, MD

❏ Use a directory such as the *Trailer Life Directory for Campgrounds, RV Parks & Services* to locate campgrounds. Directories let you know campsite sizes as well as activities and facilities. They also give clear directions to campgrounds.

❏ With over 16,000 public and private campgrounds in the United States, RVers have lots of choices. Once you choose a campground, you still have some decisions to make. Some campgrounds allow campers to choose their own campsites. In addition, you'll probably be asked whether you want full hookups or just water and electricity. Some campgrounds offer cable television hookup. Keep in mind that all these amenities will affect the price you pay.

❏ Many campgrounds near highways offer recreation rooms, swimming, hiking, perhaps a lake, and sometimes planned weekend activities. Resorts that cater to long-term residents, on the other hand, offer guests a busy calendar of daily programs—exercise, painting, music, and other activities. Often a full-time leader plans social events.

❏ Keep all your campground membership cards together in the glove compartment so they're handy when you register at a campground. Also, you won't have to carry them in your billfold or purse.

❏ If your travel schedule is such that you arrive early at a campground, let the office staff know that you will not stay longer than 24 hours overall.

❏ Most campgrounds have a night registration procedure so that if you arrive after the office is closed, you can choose a site and pay in the morning.

❑ If a campground is full and you cannot camp in an overflow area, ask the office staff to refer you to another campground that has space.

❑ Expect to find places without full hookups. Know how to boondock, or dry camp (camp without any hookups). Always keep a sufficient supply of fresh water and leave empty space in the gray and black water tanks.

❑ Before you level your RV, make sure the cord and hoses can reach the electricity, water, and sewer hookups.

❑ On a cold night, if the hose to the RV from the campground spigot freezes, detach it and put it into the shower to thaw.

❑ Sometimes in larger resorts, especially if many of the units stay parked for an extended period, an LP gas truck will deliver gas directly to the sites. Let the office staff know if you're interested in delivery.

❑ Laundry may not be your favorite task on vacation, but you'll nearly always find the campground laundry is clean and well maintained. Campground owners want to make sure their laundry facilities are given high ratings in campground directories. Usually laundries are busiest during the evening hours.

❑ Consider joining a local camping group that camps together perhaps once a month during the camping season in your area. It's a great way to meet congenial people, make new friends, and learn about RVing.

❑ On soggy ground, avoid using metal jacks to level the RV since they will sink deeper in mud than the tires.

❏ Before you leave a campground, be sure to turn off the water *pump* switch and the water *heater* switch in your RV. The water pump switch has an automatic on/off pressure switch. If it malfunctions, causing the pump to operate without actually pumping water, the pump's bearing could be damaged. Since the water heats up quickly when you need it, you'll save propane by turning it off when you're traveling.

❏ Check your turn signals and lights before you leave and make sure you have at least one-fourth of a tank of fresh water on board.

❏ Before you hit the road, take a quick look around the RV's interior to be sure everything is stowed. Check screw tops on jars (especially those in the refrigerator) occasionally to make sure they're still tightly closed. That way you'll be able to enjoy yourself at your next destination instead of mopping up items that spilled or broke.

———— ◇ ————

Campground Broadcast

OSAGE BEACH, MISSOURI, nestles up to the "Big Dragon," an apt name for the Lake of the Ozarks, whose shape is reminiscent of a fiery serpent. The lake was formed in 1931 when Bagnell Dam was constructed on the Osage River, which created the new economy of tourism in central Missouri. The lake area offers boating, water-skiing, fishing, golfing, amusement centers, caves, specialty shops, factory outlets, malls, and entertainment with some of the best musicians and comedians in the state. The lake area has more than 100 restaurants with menus ranging from continental cuisine to Ozark barbecue and fish to home-style cooking to buffets and quick burgers.

It was a radiant Sunday morning at the Osage Beach RV Park when Paul went outside to look over the motorhome. The night before, during our hasty trek to Osage Beach, we had driven over a raked, uneven road with major bumps.

During the morning I talked by telephone with Dave Sprague, a radio host, who confirmed the time for our radio broadcast on KRMS from the campground the next day. I talked with the staff at the campground office to be sure all was clear with them about the broadcast.

After lunch, Paul went with Lib and John in the tow car to a nearby Wal-Mart. While they were gone, I straightened up the motorhome, swept the ceramic tile parts of the floor, and vacuumed the carpeted parts with a hand-held cleaner. A few spots of grease remained on the carpet from the foot traffic at Dale's Diesel the day before. But I considered them happy reminders of finding our engine problem, getting on the road again, and arriving at the campground in time for the radio broadcast scheduled before we left home.

I had begun to review information for the radio interview when Paul and the Graybeals returned from shopping. Carefully controlling his enthusiasm about his purchases, Paul unrolled two large green-and-cream-colored throw rugs, one for the carpeted area between the two sofas at the front of the motorhome and the other for the ceramic tiled dining/kitchen floor. Lib had helped to select them. They looked just right in every way. He then showed me a new pair of shoes to replace ones that had gotten greasy from the diesel engine episode. Lastly, he pulled from a RadioShack bag two two-way radio transceivers. He called them "communicators." With clear instruction, he promptly told me how to work one and took the other outside.

I heard mine buzz, pressed the button, and talked into it. Then I released the button, and I heard Paul reply. Satisfied, Paul returned and placed the communicators on the dashboard. Paul loves electronics and thought these might come in handy on our trip.

The next morning about 8:30, John drove Paul and me in the tow car to Kenilworth's Bakery. It was clear and about 65 degrees but promised to get into the 90s by the afternoon. John and Lib had scouted out the bakery and a restaurant the night before when they went to dinner. I bought a dozen fresh assorted buns to offer to the radio people along with coffee and soft drinks.

Lib would make the coffee since she and John had an electric coffee maker that they used daily. I did not carry one with me because Paul did not drink coffee at all and I drank very little. I did plan to install a coffee maker for guests when I found one that attached under the counter above either the sink or dining table.

Shortly after 10 o'clock, Dave Sprague and Ed Foxmier, radio hosts for KRMS 1150, pulled in behind our motorhome in their white radio-station van. The temperature was already in the 80s, and they had rushed over from another remote broadcast location. I offered them a cold soda, which Dave accepted. We talked as they hurriedly set up their remote equipment. Soon they had placed several pieces of electronic gear, a wind-protected microphone, and a headset on the gray, unpainted wooden picnic table beside our motorhome.

For the broadcast of "The Morning Magazine," Dave put the headset on his almost clean-shaven head and placed a microphone in front of me as we sat on the same side of the picnic table. Across from us perched Lib, John, and Paul. Ed stood near a small satellite dish and also wore a headset. He served as the technical liaison with the studio.

On the table in front of the radio equipment lay a copy of the campground brochure. At my left was my three-ringed notebook with its paper information pages in clear plastic sleeves so that I could turn them if needed without making noise.

Before we knew it, Dave announced the program—we were on the air. A young man of football-player build, Dave possessed the gifts that set apart radio hosts—a facility for wit and words and a congenial personality to match. In that casual setting, Dave asked good questions that would interest and benefit his listeners. A nice breeze fanned us as we talked.

When one of Dave's questions seemed appropriate for one of my cohorts, I moved the mike across the table. Lib told an anecdote about how I take notes and put their pictures in an album for them. John talked about how he started RV travel in a homemade trailer and about his experience in the campground business. Paul told about converting the washer/dryer area of the motorhome into a desk area. I was proud of the way each of them rose to the occasion.

The show ran about 40 minutes. After Dave and Ed signed off, we invited them to see our motorhome. Inside, we took them on a tour and served the buns and coffee. Both Dave and Ed are very able speakers. They love what they do and it shows. Both are young and from Missouri, Dave from Columbia and Ed from Jefferson City. They told me that their third host, Mike Anthony, was back at the station.

As we sat and talked we told them the story behind the grease spots on the carpet. A former "carpet man" before becoming a radio talk show host, Ed said that Spot Shot would take out the grease with no problem.

After a great visit and a few photographs, and with the remaining buns in hand, Dave and Ed packed up their equipment and returned to the studio to share the food with the crew there.

About 12:30 or so, still feeling the exhilaration of our morning experience, Lib, Paul, and I rode in the tow car with John at the wheel. Dave and Ed had suggested some sights to see in the area, so we headed toward them and turned at the sign for the Bagnell Dam Scenic Overlook. From a parking area, we walked in 96-degree heat beneath a huge oak tree to the nearby overlook. Below was the dam itself and to our right was the beginning of the lake. Signs at the overlook helped us to pinpoint various features of the landscape and historical points.

As we left the parking lot, I saw that it was possible to drive down to the dam itself. We opted to turn left, however, retracing our route, crossing SR 54, and passing a white-and-blue sign to Willmore Lodge.

Leaving our air-conditioned car, we walked in the stifling hot sun up a roadway toward the rustic Adirondack-style rambling complex of Western pine logs on a foundation of local stone and concrete. We opened the door to the foyer of Willmore Lodge and saw ahead a huge two-story reception room with a fireplace. Formerly used by Union Electric as an administrative and entertainment center, the lodge now houses a museum and cultural activities center as well as the office of the Lake Area Chamber of Commerce.

We visited the museum, returned to the adjacent reception room, and then walked outside to a porch and balcony that overlooked the Lake of the Ozarks. As I stood there gazing at the water that extended beyond the horizon, a speedboat almost silently left a fanning wake in the calm blue lake. My muscles and spirit began to relax. I realized that with the radio appointment completed, I could become a tourist—my favorite form of recreation.

4

Using Electronic Equipment
on the Road

TRAVELING IN an RV used to mean "getting away from it all." These days, people are more likely to take it all with them: televisions, CD players, e-mail, computers, and more. Technology has made RV travel more enjoyable, convenient, and safe. Here are some ideas that RVers say work for them.

❏ If you like electronics, try these tips:
  • A wireless doorbell from Lowe's works well when set on the 110-volt setting.
  • Use a 12-volt fan for ventilation (instead of running the air conditioner) when dry camping.
  • To improve television reception, use RadioShack's Gold-Series Shielded Video Cable for much better reception, flexibility, and less interference. (Defective cables are the most common cause of snow, lines, and poor color.)
  • RadioShack also has a wall-mounted motion-detector infrared security system for which, when installed, many RV insurance companies will give you a discount on premiums.
  • Installing a separate speaker for CB radios gives better sound quality.

- A portable CD player with a car cassette adapter allows the enjoyment of CD music if your RV doesn't have a built-in CD player.

  —Karl M. Green, M.D.,Westminster, MD

❑ Each brand of digital camera is different, so read the owner's manual before taking a new camera on a trip. Many have found the quality of digital prints is as good as regular 35-millimeter photos. The advantage of digital is you can select what you want to print from your own computer. If you want to do your own printing on the road, you must take your own computer and printer and have the right software.

  —Lt. Col. Virginia Dillon, Alexandria, VA

❑ If your children or other passengers like to play hand-held video games on the road, purchase an inexpensive headset for each game unit so the beeps and music don't bother other people in the vehicle. (And don't forget to pack extra batteries.)

  —Steve and Debra Draper, Yorba Linda, CA

❑ You'll find all kinds of uses for two-way radio communicators. (We bought two, 2WPKTRADIO14CH38T, on sale for $69.99 each at RadioShack.)

❑ On bumpy roads, to keep your thumb from hitting the touchpad on your notebook computer by mistake, lay a piece of heavy paper or a business card over the touchpad. This will keep your thumb from accidentally touching the touchpad and yet the paper will not keep you from using the touchpad when needed.

❑ Practice until skilled with any new hardware or software *before* hitting the road. You won't have time to train as you travel.

❑ If you don't have a wireless system and you want to use e-mail on the road, use an e-mail server with a toll-free telephone number rather than a local telephone number. Many campgrounds have e-mail connections but expect you to use a toll-free number to access your server. Otherwise, you have to prevail on the office staff's good nature to hook up to their phone line and pay what they ask in toll charges. Some campgrounds may have a flat fee for this service.

❑ Take along an inexpensive multifunction fax machine. Even if you don't need it to fax something, you can use it to print from your computer and also to copy letters before you mail them.

❑ A surge protector for your computer is a must.

❑ RVers who want to watch television in a campground have several options: a standard antenna on the RV's roof that receives whatever television signals are available locally, a satellite dish, or the campground's cable hookup, which usually costs extra. Take an extra length of coaxial cable in case you need it to reach the campground's source (usually on the same post as the electricity hookup).

❑ For a small amount of money, accessory items to stabilize and aim a satellite dish properly can be purchased from the satellite dish supplier or stores such as Camping World.

❑ Here's another good reason to bring your cell phone: you can call ahead for reservations at campgrounds as you drive along, using the toll-free numbers you'll find in campground directories. This can be especially useful if you'll be arriving at the beginning of a busy weekend.

❏ When traveling in a caravan, keep in mind that CB radios
have a range, depending on the terrain and the unit itself,
of four to ten miles.

———— ◇ ————

Communicating

EVEN ON THAT damp, cloudy morning of Tuesday, Day 8 of our
trip, we rode on SR 54 from Osage Beach, Missouri, in high spirits. We headed toward Abilene, Kansas, where Paul looked forward
to once again enjoying a delicious steak at the Kirby House. He
doesn't usually eat much beef, but he had been talking about the
"best steak I ever had" that he got when we stopped at the Kirby
House several years earlier. We were on our own schedule—
no appointments to keep that day, the true freedom of traveling
by motorhome.

As we traveled and I wrote into my notebook computer, I
wondered when I would be able to check my e-mail. So far, the
campgrounds would hook me up with their modem only if my
server had an 800 number; however, my server had a local
Maryland number.

The two hand-held black communicators with their solid
three-inch antennas and protruding on/off knobs lay on the dashboard. I wondered how long it would be before we put those electronic playthings away in a drawer because we weren't using them.

We traveled on a two-lane road that undulated over the Ozark
hills like a serpent. The sun had broken through as a herd of white
cows and a few horses grazed in a meadow. We were in Hickory
County, Missouri, farming country that reminded me of home.

Lots of trees and forests, mostly deciduous with some pines
mixed in, made up much of the landscape. The trees were turning

early in Missouri, we had learned from Dave Sprague of KRMS at Osage Beach.

At almost noon, a roadside sign shouted, "Welcome to Kansas." We planned to stop for lunch when we came to a suitable parking area. We drove through Fort Scott, staying on SR 54, and shortly came upon a picnic table area, where we stopped for a pleasant lunch in our motorhomes. Afterward, Paul walked over to the Graybeals' motorhome and asked if they would be willing to try out a communicator to see what its range was. Lib and I were chosen to be the testers. It turned out that the limit was about a mile, but that was with static.

We drove all afternoon without stopping. At El Dorado we took SR 77, then traveled north to Abilene and the Covered Wagon RV Resort. It was 4:44 P.M., four hours straight of driving for John and Paul, but it had been a pleasant, scenic ride.

After hooking up to the utilities at our campsite, Paul went to the pay phone and made reservations at the Kirby House. A while later, John drove us to the restaurant for dinner.

It was fun to go back again and to see that grand historic home. The Italianate two-story house was built in 1885 by banker Thomas Kirby and subsequently turned into apartments. It had been restored into a first-class, fine dining restaurant. The hostess gave us the choice of dining downstairs or upstairs. We chose downstairs since the last time we had dined upstairs.

The main event was, of course, the moment that the server set before Paul his long-awaited steak. When he ordered, he wasn't sure whether he had filet mignon or the K.C. Strip Steak on our earlier trip. After eating the 12-ounce strip steak and a small portion of my filet mignon, he decided that he'd had the filet before, but he enjoyed his meal nevertheless. As for me, I have never eaten such a tender, savory filet or enjoyed such delicious mashed potatoes and beef gravy.

We all splurged on desserts, and I declared I would not be able to eat another dessert for two days. I had a very generous serving of apple cobbler, but I ate every delicious bite!

After dinner, Paul smiled broadly and his eyes twinkled as I took his picture standing at the white picket fence that framed the lawn of the Kirby House. We knew we would gladly go out of our way to dine in that restaurant again.

That night at the campground, Richard and Catherine (Cathy) Osborn, the owners, helped me to retrieve my e-mail. I explained to Richard that I would gladly pay the toll charge and would time the minutes that I was on the Internet. Cathy patiently helped me to get online. I downloaded the e-mail, read it, and disconnected. New to this procedure, I thought I had to read my e-mails while I was hooked up to the Internet, so I hurriedly scanned all of the messages. That took just under eight minutes. Richard said that I owed him $1.80. I gladly paid him and added a little extra. He and Cathy could not have been more helpful. Later, Paul reminded me that once the e-mail is in my notebook, I can open and read it, which I did.

On a sunshiny Wednesday morning, Day 9, John and Lib left the Covered Wagon RV Resort—Lib in the Honda, John in the motorhome. John was having their motorhome lubricated and Lib wanted to scout out antique shops in Abilene. They would meet at the Eisenhower Center later. John planned to call us on the CB when they were ready for us to meet them there to continue our trip west.

On a previous trip with the Graybeals, we had toured the Eisenhower Center at S.E. Fourth Street in Abilene. So the Graybeals and we were familiar with the place to meet that morning.

Paul and I did "catch-up" tasks in and around the motorhome. Paul drained the water/fuel separator, then he unhooked our motorhome's electric cable, water hose, and sewer hose from the campground utilities so that we would be ready to leave the campsite.

I brought my travel logs up to date and placed the computer on a folding table beside the navigator's seat in preparation for the day's travel. Then I headed for the campground's pay telephone. Since I had several calls to make, I carried one of the new communicators in case Paul got a CB message from John that he and Lib were ready for us to meet them.

As I walked on the chipped-stone road of the campground toward the telephone, I was surprised to see Lib drive toward me in the Honda. She lowered the driver's window as I walked up to her. She said that John had not been able to raise us on the CB and that he was in the parking lot at the Eisenhower Center. We were to meet him there.

"Okay," I said. On an impulse, I handed Lib the communicator. "Here. You might need this."

I hurried back to the motorhome. As we were leaving the campground, we got a message on the CB from John. He had left the Eisenhower Center, he said, and was getting gas for the motorhome.

Using the communicator, I called Lib, who had driven back to the Eisenhower Center by that time. She said anxiously that she did not know where John was. I reassured her that we had just heard from him on the CB.

When we arrived at the center's parking area, we noticed Lib on the opposite side of the large visitor building from where we were parking. John was on a nearby street heading toward us. He said on the CB that he did not know where Lib was. Paul told him we could see her coming around to join us.

About 10:30 A.M., reunited at last, the Graybeals and we pulled away from the Eisenhower Center in Abilene, heading across Kansas.

"Well, I must say those communicators certainly proved themselves," I said to Paul.

With his eyes on the road, he said matter-of-factly, "I thought they might come in handy."

5

Getting Along:
Relationships on the Road

NO TWO people look alike, think alike, or travel alike—at least not most of the time. It's a wonder that we get along at all! Yet when traveling in an RV, we must try to maintain smooth relationships with all of our fellow travelers because we're "stuck" together for the duration of the trip. The tips in this chapter will help you to avoid turning little annoyances into big problems.

❑ When hosting another couple in the same RV on a trip, limit the amount of luggage each person brings because of the storage space available. It also helps if the trip is new to everyone so that all are interested in stopping to see the sights and experiencing the adventure for the first time.
—Bonnie Talbert, New Windsor, MD

❑ Being together day and night in a small space demands patience, a determination to understand and accept each other, and sometimes real effort to be funny and compatible. Be ready to keep learning about each other, no matter how long you've known each other.

❑ Freedom is basic to camping—freedom to relax, or to shop, or to cook, or to read, or to eat in your own vehicle, or to stay inside when others sit at a group campfire, or to sleep late, or to sightsee. Camping is vacation. Try not to infringe on the freedom of others in your group.

❑ When you have mechanical or other problems, keep the other people in your group informed as much as possible. When everyone knows what's going on, they can understand and support the person with the problem.

❑ When traveling with friends, just as when traveling with your spouse or children, be willing to give and take, be willing to accommodate and accept, be generous and gracious and courteous. Concentrate on the good points of your traveling companions.

❑ If you are following a leader, refrain from telling the leader what to do. Instead, offer encouragement and support.

❑ A simple thank-you builds good relations. For example, thank your friends for waiting for you if you have been delayed at a rest area or looking for booklets at a welcome center.

❑ Speak slowly and distinctly into the CB. It helps the other person to understand better.

❑ If you're normally the leader, be open to letting someone else try planning and navigating. You may learn something new yourself.

❑ Before a trip with friends, discuss what each of you wants to include in your trip. It's good to actually write down an itinerary, even if it is tentative and you change destinations as you travel.

❑ Agree upon who will lead and who will follow as you travel on the road. You can take turns or one person may do all of the leading. The leader should let the follower know by CB what's coming up, and the follower should let the leader know if traffic is backed up behind them so the leader can pull over at an appropriate, safe place to let the traffic pass.

❑ Communicate in an informative manner, sticking to the subject. Simply describe what you see. Say, "There's a truck parked on the side up ahead with a man walking beside it," instead of "Don't hit that man beside that truck."

❑ If you want to stay friends, overlook your companions' habits that bother you. One trick is to tell yourself that no one except you is perfect; therefore, as a perfect person, you can be gracious toward your imperfect fellow travelers.

❑ When caravaning, you need CB communication, of course, and should determine handles for each person using it.

❑ Consider going one way to a destination with another couple and coming back independently. That way you'll each have the satisfaction of being on your own schedule for part of the trip.

❑ It seems obvious, but tell your traveling companions about your telephone conversations that involve them. For example, when you call a friend that you all will visit, tell your traveling companions and give them any details that they need to know. This way, everyone will be on the same wavelength.

❑ Try to stick to your budget, but don't get upset if your companion spends money on something you think is frivolous—the item could have a lot of meaning to the spender, now or later, or it could just be a "mad money" expenditure. You are already saving money by RV travel, so relax about what is spent on the trip.

❑ Go where you and your companions want to go. The trip is an adventure, so if you think rock hunting is boring, but someone else wants to do it, try it.

❑ Offer options instead of making demands. Instead of saying to your travel partner, "We have to go to the grocery store after breakfast," say something such as, "Can we discuss when we can go to the grocery store next?" That way, you both have a voice in the decision.

❑ I discovered that friendships flourished on the road when we (1) talked freely with one another about plans, routes, and wishes; (2) were ready to depart on time; (3) looked on the positive side of what could be taken as negative words or incidents; (4) thanked one another for courtesies or work; (5) were willing to sightsee or follow a route that others chose; (6) helped to research places to see and things to do; (7) shared expenses willingly; (8) laughed or saw the funny side of words or happenings; (9) were willing to jump in and help with knowledge or labor as needed; and (10) accepted the other persons as they were, not as we thought they should be. The idea is for all to share in the jobs and joys of the trip together.

❑ Remember that in the RV lifestyle, domestic duties know no gender. Everybody pitches in wherever necessary.

———— ◇ ————

The Romantic Old West

ON EACH TRIP west, I find myself looking for something that puts me in touch with the Old West of my imagination—the West that I envisioned when I was a fourth grade farm girl singing "Home on the Range" in music class, the West that my father read about in Zane Grey novels, the West that Gene Autry sang about in "Back in the Saddle Again"—something that would satisfy a deep yearning within me. I had found it on a previous trip as I wandered through the ProRodeo Hall of Fame and Museum in Colorado Springs, Colorado. But so far on the current trip, the touch of the romantic West had eluded me.

Our two-motorhome caravan had left Abilene, Kansas, on I-70. We had driven due west across the state as far as Oakley, Kansas, that Wednesday. By nine o'clock the next day, a summery Thursday, we were back on I-70, moving toward Exit 438 east of Burlington, Colorado, where we would turn north.

We drove on a straight highway toward a cloudless blue sky in that wide open prairie of parched grasses, cornfields, soybeans, and plowed ground. The grassy median strip and wide shoulders looked thirsty in their blonde crew cuts. No bushes protruded from the "scalp." We passed Colby, Kansas. Traffic was light and the road was bumpy where it was patched.

Sometimes the four of us rode along for miles without communicating. We used the CB only occasionally to ask a question or give a comment or plan what to do next.

"Welcome to Wonderful Colorado" a roadside sign beamed at us a little after 10 o'clock. Just inside the border, at Burlington, we left I-70 for SR 385 north. We continued on the level prairie that is the apron to the Rocky Mountains to the west. A few Kansas sunflowers with small blooms grew alongside the highway.

It seemed isolated and remote. I could see how pioneers must have felt all alone as they laboriously traveled across those great expanses of land.

The countryside changed from level farmland to mildly rolling rocky terrain covered with low grasses and sagebrush. Paul stopped at the side of the road to let a couple of trucks go past. Cattle grazed on the hillsides; some lay down in the sunshine.

We passed a large dairy operation with a corral of buffalo and Holsteins. A little farther on, a long snake of irrigation pipe sprayed water from beneath its silver skeleton across a field.

As we passed a huge cattle lot, I blinked and sat upright. To my right side, three cowboys rode horses, loping on the dirt paths between the corrals in the feedlots on a hillside. Real working cowboys! They weren't out on the range, but they were riding horses and wearing ten-gallon hats.

After spending the night in Cheyenne, Wyoming, the next morning we continued on I-25 northwest toward Casper. I kept looking for more evidence of Western culture. We saw deer and more deer—in fact, a herd of them. Cattle grazed on dry-looking ranges with green clumps of sagebrush. We passed flat mesas and buttes with rocky cliffs. Modest one-story homes hugged the ranges. A lone clump of blooming pink wildflowers outside my window put a smile on my face. The Laramie Mountain Range stood on our left in the distance. The North Laramie River cradled only a small stream in its rocky bed. Fish Creek contained only rocks and gravel—definitely no fish!

As we ate lunch at a parking area along the highway, John said that the best view of the Grand Tetons was as you came down from the north. And so after lunch, we continued on a northwesterly route.

The Rattle Snake Range of mountains appeared on our left in the distance. We passed Natrona, elevation 5,610 feet. Under a cloudless blue sky, we rode through a mid-September landscape of straw-like grass, sagebrush, a few goldenrods, and some black-eyed Susans blooming by the roadside.

After stopping for a half-hour in a long line of traffic caused by a fire in a pickup truck, we continued on SR 20 through range country and through Shoshoni. Then we drove down into Wind River Canyon. We were greeted by impressive red and tan rocks of the steep-sided canyon, the Bighorn River, and railroad tracks and another road in the canyon. Clusters of evergreen shrubs clung to the steep rocky mountainside. We passed through three short tunnels, and the road wound around the canyon floor. I marveled at views of the canyon.

The blue-green Bighorn River flowed swiftly as it and the railroad track continued through the mountain canyon. A huge boulder and many smaller ones rested in the river as if they had fallen off the mountainsides. Guard rails lined the roadside next to the river. The tops of the canyon walls were too high to see from my seat.

In Thermopolis, we refueled and headed out once again into range country on County Road 120, marked as a scenic route on our map. The two-lane, paved road was smooth with a center yellow line and white side lines—a pleasant one on which to drive.

Through my right window, I saw steep, eroded rocks and rock strata. It's amazing what nature does to itself—wind and water carve out rock statues much as a sculptor chisels out works of art from stone. I felt as if we were traveling through a museum of landscape art.

One weathered rock ledge evoked thoughts of Egyptian pyramids and sphinxes. Another huge rock formation resembled the giant *Titanic* or, as we got closer, a medieval castle with bulwarks. Two rocks eroded in a bank of soil looked like a woman's droopy eyelids. An exposed series of smooth rocks looked like a giant elephant's foot.

On the surface, the area appeared desolate, but I'm sure there was much unseen life among the sagebrush, in the gullies and canyons, and on the dirt roads. I wouldn't want to live among those rocks and gullies, although cattle grazed on the slopes of dried grass and sagebrush.

As we drove down a fairly steep hill into Cody, I began to sense an excitement about the Old West. With a population of almost 8,000, the town was founded in 1896 by Colonel William F. Cody, otherwise known as "Buffalo Bill" for his expertise in hunting buffalo. We wound our way through Cody to the Ponderosa Campground. It was a little after six o'clock. To Lib's and my delight, we decided to eat out.

After settling in at our campsites, John and Lib unhooked the tow car, and the four of us went to the Irma Restaurant for dinner. The restaurant was on the first floor of the Irma Hotel, built by Buffalo Bill for $80,000 and named for his daughter. We entered through plate-glass front doors and soon stood looking into a huge dining room, noisy with music and hundreds of diners chatting.

Along one wall was an elaborately carved cherry wood bar built in France for $100,000. It was a gift to Colonel Cody in 1900 by Queen Victoria to show her appreciation of his command performance. The bar was shipped by steamer to New York, then by rail to Red Lodge, Montana, and then by horse-drawn freight wagon to Cody.

Around the walls near the high ceiling hung animal trophies—buffalo, elk, moose, deer, and others. In between were large oil paintings framed with ornate gilt frames. The ceiling itself was a pressed tin pattern. Above our table hung an antler chandelier.

The room was filled with patrons, some wearing cowboy hats, some with Western jeans, some bearded, some apparently

tourists as we were. My tourist information guide said that since the early 1900s, the Irma had been a meeting place for cattlemen, oilmen, and sheepherders. As we ate, a man wearing a cowboy hat played country music on a keyboard.

Without my knowledge, my dear husband stopped on his way to the food bar and asked the man at the keyboard to play "Red River Valley" or any other Gene Autry song for me. He put $1 in the tip jar. The musician had set the keyboard to sound like a guitar. A thrill went through me when I heard one of my favorite songs.

With the real Western milieu, my favorite kind of country music, the delicious food, the history of the room itself, a swift and pleasant server, and congenial company at the table, it was a special moment. As John would say, we "made a memory."

Back at the campground, we decided that the next morning we would sightsee in downtown Cody. Afterward, we would move on to Yellowstone National Park and from there to the Grand Tetons.

On Saturday morning, Day 12, after I received and sent e-mail at the campground office, the four of us set out for the Buffalo Bill Historical Center at 730 Sheridan Avenue. Happily, it was just a few blocks from the Ponderosa Campground and had space in its large parking area for RVs.

The tour booklet said we should plan on a minimum of four hours to visit the center. Knowing that checkout time at the campground was 11 A.M. and that we might be longer than that at the center, we unhooked from the utilities and met with our motorhomes at the center.

Paul said he wanted to wash the windshield and adjust the placement of the passenger side-view mirror rather than tour the center. (I had learned not to push him into doing something just because I thought he should do it. Just as I have likes and dislikes, so does he. He respects mine and I have learned to respect his.) So I walked with Lib and John to the nearby entrance to the center. A brochure described the various museums and showed their locations—the Plains Indian Museum, the Buffalo Bill Museum, the Whitney Gallery of Western Art, the Cody Firearms Museum, and the McCracken Research Library. Lib and I chose the Whitney Gallery of Western Art and the Buffalo Bill Museum.

Since Lib and I had taken oil painting lessons from Shirley Lippy, a prominent local artist, we headed first to see the art. John wanted to visit the Cody Firearms Museum and the Buffalo Bill Museum. We would meet in an hour at the front desk area.

Lib and I entered the Whitney Gallery and made our way admiringly through an exhibition of local art to the rear of the gallery. There the works of Charles M. Russell and Frederic Remington drew gasps of awe from us both. The scenes depicted in Russell's massive oil painting of a buffalo hunt and his other oils of Western life looked real. What skill he showed in bringing the West to his canvas. I found that Remington's bronze sculptures were more detailed than Russell's and his oils more impressionistic.

On our way out of the gallery, I paused at a display of open books that I had missed seeing on the way in. One was *The Desert of Wheat* by Zane Grey. I admired the frontispiece, illustrated by W. H. D. Koerner.

We could have lingered, but we had already spent three-fourths of an hour. We wanted to visit the Buffalo Bill Museum. As Lib and I crossed the Orientation Gallery, we met John. He had completed his visits and said he would wait for us there.

We walked into the entrance of the Buffalo Bill Museum. On my right, a series of time lines on the wall showed Bill's life in context with other happenings in the United States. The chart was printed in large letters and was unusually easy to read and follow. What a great man Buffalo Bill was. In addition to his reputation as a buffalo hunter and Wild West Show entrepreneur, he ran a newspaper, advocated women's rights, encouraged conservation, and was very much against the slaughter of buffalo merely for their hides.

I looked into showcases displaying his clothing, guns, saddles, and family artifacts. I stood in front of his beaded and fringed buckskin jacket, which sported "eagle" shoulder boards that identified his rank of colonel and aide-de-camp to the governor. I drew in my breath at the painting by Rosa Bonheur of Colonel Cody on a trotting white stallion in a pastoral scene. I admired his handsome brown leather saddle with angora serape, bridle, and beaded gauntlets. I walked around the yellow stagecoach with a red interior that was used in his Wild West Show during the skit "Attack on the Deadwood Stage Coach."

In addition to the memorabilia of Colonel Cody, the museum displayed both fancy and everyday pieces of Western culture, from a red felt sombrero to a cookstove with a tin coffeepot and cast-iron skillets used on the range.

I returned to the entrance area to read again the words of a wall placard: "The cowboy is a mythic character in America. We admire him for his independence, his honesty, his modesty, and courage."

To take some of the Old West with me, I bought a book about the Buffalo Bill Museum. I also found a CD of Gene Autry singing my favorites, "You Are My Sunshine," "Back in the Saddle Again," and "Have I Told You Lately That I Love You."

The three of us walked out of the center and across the parking lot to our motorhomes. As Paul and I prepared and ate lunch, he told me what he had accomplished on the motorhome, for which I thanked him. I've learned that he likes to be appreciated and thanked for his work, even if it is something that he normally would do on his own. I told him about the museum, and he was pleased that I liked it. With my yearning to experience the romantic West fulfilled, our small caravan drove out of Cody toward the Grand Tetons.

6

Travel Courtesy, Travel Comfort

Y OU MAY be on vacation, but don't leave your manners at home. When you extend these simple courtesies to other travelers, they'll respond in kind. In addition, you'll find life on the road and in campgrounds is more comfortable and enjoyable when you use these tips.

Travel Courtesy

❑ Don't run your generator (or vehicle engine itself) and appliances all night long or early in the morning. Consider that in "mixed-use" campgrounds, you are sharing the area with tent campers. Most people who use campgrounds are there to enjoy some peace and quiet and to commune with nature. Noisy generators and loud televisions ruin the experience.

—David Iler, Cyberwest, Denver, CO

❑ Slow down when driving on dirt campground roads so you don't raise too much dust for campers or for any vehicles following you. Also, although the children in your group may love shuffling in the dirt, stirring up big clouds of dust, remind them to do that far away from where people are camping.

—Louie and Kiyo Shiroma, Culver City, CA

- ❏ Have a friendly attitude toward other drivers, whatever their vehicles. Give them the benefit of the doubt when it comes to their motives. Road rage/revenge leads to tragedy.

- ❏ Mind your manners wherever you roam. People everywhere appreciate a "please" and "thank you."

- ❏ Be sure to ask if guests would like to see the inside of your vehicle. We all like to see how other people camp. It gives us new ideas for our own RVs.

- ❏ Never dump except at a dump station or a sewer connection at a campsite.

- ❏ Honor the campground's checkout time. Someone may be waiting for your campsite.

- ❏ Be aware that using the auxiliary generator at rest stops stirs up dust outside the RV. Other travelers who are trying to eat their lunches may not appreciate it.

- ❏ When you're traveling in a caravan, stay at least a quarter of a mile behind the RV in front of you. It gives the leader room to maneuver in case of stopped traffic or unexpected road conditions, and it gives people passing you a chance to get in and out of your lane. More space between the RVs also gives you a broader view of the countryside.

- ❏ Try to go with the flow of traffic, unless it's over the speed limit.

- ❏ When three or more vehicles are backed up behind you and road conditions permit, pull onto the shoulder to let traffic pass.

❑ Blink your headlights when a trucker passes you to let the driver know that it's safe to pull back into the lane. At night, flash your high beams for the same purpose. When the driver gives you a double wink with the lights, it means "thank you."

❑ When you park on the street, make sure you aren't blocking anyone's way.

❑ When you're staying with friends, use your calling card when you make calls on their phone.

Travel Comfort

❑ Most RV mattresses aren't as comfortable as your bed at home. Adding an eggshell foam mattress, placed with the smooth side up, makes sleeping more comfortable.
—Louis and Ann Beeler, Salome, AZ

❑ To decrease the heat/cold transmitted through the bath skylight, solar windshield covers for cars can be trimmed and attached with Velcro. Clean the area for the Velcro with rubbing alcohol to increase the adhesiveness.
—Karl M. Green, M.D., Westminster, MD

❑ If your bed mattress shifts on its wood platform while you're traveling over bumpy roads and during sudden stops, place a piece of rubberized matting between the platform and the mattress. This will eliminate your having to push the mattress back into position after a day's travel. You can buy the matting at carpet stores and RV dealers.

❑ When riding through monotonous rocky formations that go on for miles, challenge your and your children's imaginations to identify images such as cathedrals, whales, or pyramids. Or if a highway runs on for miles lined with trees, look for hues of green and other colors, textures, shadows, and lines as if you wanted to paint the details of what you see. It will bring interest and excitement to even a "dull" scene. Look for wildlife, too.

❑ Take breaks—whether that means stopping at a rest area, taking a walk along the beach, or having lunch.

❑ Be sure to include some no-travel days. Don't try to crowd too many miles or activities into the time available. You need time to rest and catch up with chores (and yourself).

❑ A shopping center or Wal-Mart parking lot is a good place for a rest stop on a secondary road that does not have designated rest or picnic areas.

❑ Passengers can do many things to keep from getting bored during a long day of travel: do handiwork such as knitting or crocheting or cross-stitching, listen to the radio, play games that don't distract the driver, write in a journal, browse tour books and maps, or listen to audiobooks from the library (with a headset, if desired). You may even voluntarily give the driver a neckrub or backrub. Sitting still and putting off doing an activity creates fatigue and boredom.

❑ Don't let fatigue creep up on you. If you find yourself feeling run down, a good nap may be just what you need to restore your body and spirit.

❑ If you depend on having your hair or nails done regularly on the road, you'll probably get good results at well-known beauty salon chains in shopping malls. Or ask for recommendations at campground offices. Have your stylist at home write out any special instructions.

❑ When you stay at a campground for several days running, you can stay hooked up to the sewer site and let the gray water run into it instead of into the RV's holding tank. The result? A nice long shower without worrying that the tank will fill up and let gray water back up into the shower.

❑ If you find the curtains in the bedroom don't make the room dark enough, try hanging heavy towels over them until you get home and can fix the problem with heavier lining material or new curtains.

❑ If you're concerned that the dash air conditioner takes too much power away from the motor, use the auxiliary generator to run the overhead air conditioner instead.

❑ Who knows what weather you'll be traveling through today? Dress in layers so you can adjust to changing conditions.

❑ If the RV's propane furnace doesn't keep your rig toasty warm enough when you're parked at a site, try a small electric heater with a thermostat.

❑ One of the great features about RV travel is that you can visit friends or relatives along the way and still sleep in your own bed—because it's parked in the driveway.

———— ◇ ————

Yellowstone and the Grand Tetons

ON A HOT, bright Saturday early afternoon, after visiting the superb Buffalo Bill Historical Center in Cody, we headed for Yellowstone National Park.

Along the scenic highway, we came to a road construction area where the pavement ended, drove onto rough packed dirt and gravel, and crept along at 10 miles per hour. We bounced, rocked, and shimmied in accordance with the bumps, ditches, and accordion surface. Paul and John talked on the CB to keep each other informed about what was in front of and behind our caravan.

We drove under the narrow entrance to the park at 2:21 P.M., following a paved road with a double yellow center line and white lines on each side. The idyllic road turned into "Road construction ahead—extremely rough road." At a high altitude, the rough road wound around the side of a mountain. It was hard to keep my fingers on the laptop keys. The lowering sun cast shadows of lodgepole pine trees and lit up patches on the forest floor's dried grassy mat and graying logs.

By 4:30 P.M., we were parallel parking into Site A41 of the Grant Village Campground in Yellowstone National Park. Paul nestled our motorhome among tall pines. That area of the park was somewhere between 6,500 and 8,500 feet above sea level.

We would be boondocking that evening. A lot of national parks do not offer utility service, but of course, the cost is less for a campsite. While the average fee for a campground site with hookups is about $23.00, the Yellowstone site was $16.00. With our Golden Eagle Passport, that fee was reduced to $7.95. Yellowstone has 11 park campgrounds. The Fishing Bridge RV Park has

340 RV sites with full hookups that cost $30.24 per night (with no reduction for a Golden Eagle Passport).

After turning on the auxiliary generator to provide electricity for the microwave, we ate dinner in the motorhome. It was almost seven o'clock when we joined John and Lib in their tow car to sightsee the area. We headed for Old Faithful, the famous geyser.

Driving on the park roads, we came upon a "bear jam," as John called it. Vehicles were parked askew on both sides of the road and people were walking along the road and across it. A brown bear only about 30 feet into the woods calmly nosed at something on the forest floor. Lib and I also went to look more closely but we did not linger because we feared the bear might decide to run toward us.

We passed the Continental Divide at 8,391 feet and began to see other wildlife from the car—two female elk, a male elk with huge antlers, more females and yearlings, and buffalo.

We found our way to Old Faithful and joined other tourists sitting or standing in front of the geyser—at a safe distance, of course. After only about 10 minutes, the geyser began its activity. First, a small spurt of water gurgled upward, then soon a higher one. Then came another and another, higher and higher each time. White steam reached a hundred or so feet into the air.

All too soon the geyser began to subside until it was once again a low white vapor cloud at the top of a large cone-shaped base. We left the geyser area and explored the old inn with its huge, high-ceilinged lobby and stone fireplace.

When we arrived back at the campground, it was after eight o'clock. Most campgrounds have quiet hours between 8 P.M. and 8 A.M. so campers don't disturb their neighbors. That means campers may not run their auxiliary generators to use the microwave or other appliances. In our motorhome, we could use only the coach lights that were absolutely necessary because the power for those lights came from the coach battery, which we did not want to run down.

The next morning, Sunday, I got up at 5:30 to write in my laptop journal. It was dark and the coach was shivering cold. I zipped up a fleece jacket over my pajamas and used a sweater to cover my knees as I sat at the dinette table. I tried to type into the laptop computer using only the light from the screen and the light from the bathhouse across the road, but I found it was impossible. I turned on one small light above my left shoulder. I did not turn on the furnace in order to save propane, which was needed to run the refrigerator. My fingers were cold. I was not a happy boondocker. There I was in that elegant coach, living like it was a lean-to.

I had worked about an hour when I felt the vehicle shaking. Paul was getting up. He, too, was cold, so I asked if we could turn on the furnace. He moved the thermostat lever to On, and wonderful warm air flowed from the heat vents. I looked at the thermometer we had put outside on our coach steps the night before. At 7:42 A.M., it said 42 degrees!

At 8:01, we turned on the auxiliary generator that supplied 120 volts to the various outlets in the coach, energy for the re-frigerator and other appliances. That allowed us to turn on the heat pump, which used electricity, and turn off the furnace, which used propane.

I sat in the passenger seat with my laptop hooked up to electricity. How good it was to once again have all our creature comforts!

Looking back, I could have turned on the furnace without asking my husband when I got up that morning and I could have used the necessary lights above the dinette table. Our reason for conserving propane was that we didn't know when we could get a refill. As for the lights, I learned later from Paul that our coach battery would be recharged by the auxiliary generator through an onboard converter as we drove down the highway. We usually turned on the generator to furnish electricity to my laptop computer or the air conditioner. The next time we boondock, I will be better informed about what I can do without having to ask my traveling companion.

At 8:37 A.M. our small caravan moved out of the campground in light rain. Soon we headed south on SR 89, a two-lane, paved road, toward my long-awaited view of the Grand Tetons. The road led through a lodgepole pine forest with its tall, straight, skinny tree trunks; across the Continental Divide at 7,988 feet; and through both living forests and burned areas with naked, ghostly tree trunks.

Leaving Yellowstone, we entered the John D. Rockefeller, Jr., Memorial Parkway. The rain continued as we crossed the Snake River.

Unceremoniously, we entered Grand Teton National Park at 9:26 A.M. After riding a few minutes, I looked up from my laptop computer. Straight ahead, over the tops of pine trees in the gray-white mist, protruded the lone peak of a mountain. I sat up straighter and peered closer. Jackson Lake, one of the two largest natural lakes in Wyoming, lay ahead in the mist too. We continued downhill on the two-lane, paved but rough road. Lodgepole pines, Engelmann spruces, and Douglas firs inhabited the forest on both sides.

The road curved. Across the expansive Jackson Lake, huge mountains stood waiting in the morning mist. Patches of snow filled clefts in the upper ridges. Like enormous mounds of stiffly beaten egg whites, dyed gray under those cloudy skies, the jagged peaks were silhouetted along the horizon as far as the eye could see. They were the north end of the Teton Range, a part of the Rocky Mountains, which stretch from central New Mexico to northern Alberta, Canada.

At a pullout, I stood by the shore of Jackson Lake holding a large black umbrella to shield my camera from the rain. A long slope of straw-like grass in shades of red, yellow, and green lay between where I stood and the water. Nearby tiny aspen trees with yellow and orange leaves brightened the morning drizzle.

Someone at the pullout told us that a good place to see the mountains was from Leeks Marina. Since the marina was not along the road and not knowing if it had ample parking and turning space for the Southwind and tow car, John and Lib decided to go on, park where they could, and wait for us. They had both been to the park before, but they encouraged us to get the most out of our short stay there.

Paul drove the Holiday Rambler down a road through woods to the large parking area of Leeks Marina. We discovered there would have been space for the Graybeals' rig and car. While Paul waited in the motorhome, I walked down toward Jackson Lake and a small office building. The young man inside was cordial and said that I could take pictures from there. He told me that Mount Moran was toward the left side of the lake. To the left and south of that mighty mountain was the Grand Teton itself, the highest peak of the Teton Range at 13,770 feet. He said that the smoke I saw across the lake low on the horizon was from a forest fire that the rangers would let burn itself out because it was not endangering anyone and there were more pressing fires elsewhere.

I sat outside on the wooden deck of the building looking toward the mountains beyond the many small motor boats on the softly lapping water. Through the mist, I began to see the colors of dried grass and reddish patches on the mountainsides. It was about 10 o'clock that Sunday morning when I said hello quietly to the Grand Tetons.

Paul drove the motorhome close by, I climbed aboard, and we soon caught up with our friends. We continued south, then turned right toward Jenny Lake and followed a route closer to the mountain range.

When we left the park, I put my computer on the floor and stood in the stairwell of the motorhome, looking out the window. To steady myself as we rode along, I held the nearby arm supports, one of which was fastened to the dashboard and the other to the passenger seat side of the motorhome. From its south side, the Grand Teton looked taupe with hints of purple, yellow, and green, in the sunshine at last. A dash of white snow covered the middle of its topmost peak. Other snow lay in nearby crevasses.

Soon the town of Jackson welcomed us with its authentic Western culture. The visitor center parking lot was too small for the Southwind and tow car to turn around in, so while Paul and I parked there, the Graybeals parked along the curb on the main street. It was lunchtime. It was also John's birthday, and Lib wanted to treat him to a nice meal.

The Wagon Wheel Restaurant was across from the visitor center and near the Graybeals' parked vehicles. The large dining room was decorated with wagon wheel chandeliers, mounted heads of elk, Western art, and a photograph by Ansel Adams of the Grand Tetons. The server told us that Jackson had 11,000 residents and that the restaurant was closed during October and November until the skiing season began in December—an annual procedure. We enjoyed our food and declined dessert. I invited John and Lib to our motorhome for a birthday dessert once we reached the campground.

We continued through Jackson, in sunshine then, on scenic SR 89 south through picturesque landscapes. The Snake River's water looked blue green as it flowed along the whitish gravel of its shores. John and Lib noticed kayakers on the river below the highway. Tall aspen trees with yellow leaves and maroon shrubs graced both sides of the highway.

Traffic was heavy—people appeared to be out enjoying the autumn colors on that brilliant Sunday afternoon. We passed through small towns, past herds of sheep and cattle, horses grazing, and spectacular, beautiful scenery. Thank you, Lord, for this feast of beauty—such a surprise to find autumn colors in mid-September here, I thought.

Wyoming became Idaho. Had it not been for the welcome sign, we would not have known the difference.

At 3:40 P.M., we drove into the Montpelier Creek KOA Kampground, Montpelier, Idaho. Lib and I did our laundry, darting back and forth between our motorhomes and the building, which also housed a game room and television set with comfortable chairs, in wind and rain.

It was Paul's idea to thaw the frozen three-layer chocolate cake in the refrigerator during that day as we traveled. To prepare for John's birthday party that evening, Paul put the extension leaf in the dinette table and retrieved the two extra matching chairs from under the bed. He had already put out the slideout in the living room area. I set the table, using the last four Happy Birthday napkins that I had on hand.

Later that evening, the Graybeals knocked at our door. Laughing and joking, we gathered at the table. I lit the tapers on the chocolate cake and we sang "Happy Birthday." With one mighty blow, John snuffed out all the candles.

I sliced and served the cake along with ice cream, a favorite dessert of John's. That delicacy, however, came in the form of pre-packaged sundaes that Paul had bought at the camp store earlier.

As I started to pull off the lid on my sundae cup, I saw that the price of 55 cents was still on the label, began to chuckle, and apologized for not taking it off. Paul kidded John and said he was going first class by spending that amount of money on him. We all laughed and enjoyed the happy moment and our time together.

After swapping stories, reminiscing, and planning our next few days' travel, we agreed to leave the campground the following morning about 8:30 and to camp near Salt Lake City the next evening. Before our friends returned to their motorhome, I thanked Lib and John once again for making it possible to include the Grand Tetons in our itinerary.

7

Getting and Staying Organized

A N RV is like a playhouse. Although getting and staying organized seems like work at home, that's not so in an RV; however, some discipline is still necessary. Lots of fellow RVers have discovered ways to make it even easier to enjoy your playhouse on the road.

❏ On your computer, make a checklist of items to always take on trips and print out a new one for each trip.

—Pete Jones, Westminster, MD

❏ When making checklists, be sure to include "one for the road": windows, vents, refrigerator, water pump—everything that should be closed, stowed, turned off, or locked. Keep it in a handy place or posted by the door. Don't forget to include the television antenna.

—Herb and Mary-Lou Pletcher, Taneytown, MD

❏ Make "reverse lists" to help with stocking perishable food for consecutive weekend trips. For the first trip of the season, plan your menus, make a shopping list, and stock the kitchen. As items are used up, list them on a shopping list in the RV. When you arrive home after a trip, move perishable items from the RV to the house and list the items as you *unpack* them. That makes stocking for the subsequent weekend easy: you won't have to remember what you left in the RV, just replace the used items and restock the items on your "unpacking" list.

—Connie Burk Davis, Westminster, MD

❑ Always have a checklist of procedures to follow when moving or parking your vehicle. Follow the procedures in a systematic way and check off each item as you go.

—Anne Carney-Brown, Finksburg, MD

❑ Use a separate set of towels and sheets of a different color from what you use at home. When you do laundry, you'll know exactly what goes back to the RV.

—Luther and Alverta Showalter, Edgewood, MD

❑ Take along a receptacle for receipts, campground maps, and other printed material that you want to keep after the trip. Keep these items in chronological order.

❑ When you take photos, take the time at that moment to write down in a small spiral tablet the time, date, place, and any other comment you want to remember about it. You'll be glad you have this information when you get your film developed and photos printed after the trip is over.

❑ Make the bed every day. An unmade bed is often visible in the rest of the RV and casts a disorganized mood over the whole interior. If the bed is made, the entire RV looks better even if dishes are piled in the sink, magazines and newspapers are strewn on the couch, and the table has things piled on it.

❑ When you begin a task, try to complete it before moving on to something else.

❑ When on a trip and you think of ideas for the RV, make a To Do list. Keep a running list of items you need to purchase so that when you have the opportunity, you know what to buy.

❑ If you're traveling and you want to remember to do something at the campground, write the task on a sticky note and stick the reminder on the dash door frame at the entry to your vehicle. You will see it as you go in or out of the vehicle.

❑ Another way of remembering something is to put an object out of its usual place. For example, placing a box of tissues on the floor can be a reminder to buy some milk when you get to the campground.

❑ In a single bag or backpack—separate from other toys and games—keep the items that your children use to entertain themselves while traveling. That way, you can easily move their special travel items from your RV to the tow car and back again.

❑ Put items away when you are finished using them. It's a simple rule but one that's easy to procrastinate about. Things that are not put away keep getting in your way, so you save time, energy, and frustration by putting items away in the first place.

❑ Never put something (especially a heavy or bulky item) on top of something else unless you want to move it in order to get to what's underneath! Whenever I "temporarily" put an object on top of another, I need the object underneath— it never fails.

❑ Standing or storing items such as books, magazines, and file folders on end takes less surface space than laying them flat and makes them easier to find.

❏ Store items near their point of first use. For example, store plates and dishes above the dinette table, and store sunglasses in a drawer near the driver's and passenger's seats.

❏ Make a list of the credit or debit cards you're taking along and the telephone numbers you need to call if they're lost or stolen. Try to limit the number of cards you take with you.

❏ Prepare an itinerary with phone numbers, dates, and places so your family and friends will know how to reach you if necessary. It also helps you feel in touch when you are far away on the road knowing that they have some idea of where you are.

❏ A plastic garbage bag in the tow vehicle or in a compartment under the RV will keep laundry out of the way until you're ready for it.

❏ When you're doing laundry in campground facilities, use the timer on your microwave to remind you when the load will be finished.

———— ◇ ————

Through Cowboy Country
to California

LIKE THE GOLD Rush '49ers, we kept heading steadily for California. At the moment, Day 14, we were in Montpelier, Idaho.

So far, we were doing a pretty good job of staying organized in our motorhome. Basically, we tried to have a place for everything and keep everything in its place. While that sounds simple, sometimes it's not.

My special responsibility was organizing the campsite diagrams, campground receipts, and memorabilia that we picked up along the way. From Day 1, I had file folders labeled "Campgrounds," "Receipts," and "Itinerary." I kept them handy by my passenger seat in a narrow wooden file box. As we made purchases, I put the receipts into the proper folder, keeping them in chronological order with a large paper clip. Each time we got a campsite diagram, I wrote on it the date that we camped and put it in chronological order in a separate file folder.

When Paul was having a problem remembering what was in which basement compartment, he made an inventory list. I made a file folder called "Inventory" and put it in the wooden box so the list would be easily available.

For other materials that we collected along the way, we used a corrugated cardboard storage box that I put in the wardrobe. I made a file folder for each geographic area as we collected something from it. That kept booklets, brochures, and newspapers from being scattered around the motorhome.

I had to discipline myself to update a travel log with the day's expenses and mileage every evening. It was so easy to put it off, but I found that putting it off to another day only made the next day's entries more complicated. So the lesson I learned was to do the travel log entries each day (or at least the first thing the next morning).

The drive continued to be beautiful—a canyon with a small winding stream flowing beside the road and heavy, thick bushes changing colors to yellow and red from green of various shades, Black Angus and red cattle in open range areas, stands of white- and gray-trunked Aspen trees, red hillside soil that looked even more crimson with flaming red and coral bushes near the top of the mountainside, and sheer rock faces. We followed SR 89 through Logan, Utah, to Brigham City, where we took I-15 south to Salt Lake City.

While riding along, Paul and I sometimes thought of items we wanted to purchase when we got to a store. I've learned to keep a running list on a memo pad so that when we actually go to the store we'll remember to get the items.

We arrived at Camp VIP, Salt Lake City, at 1:20 P.M. The nice wide sites with 50-amp service, cable television, and space to put out the slideout made for pleasant living.

We immediately drove to GenPlus where a very congenial man replaced the generator air filter and oil filters. Paul bought a spare oil filter and kept the used air filter, which was not very dirty. I made notes because he planned to start a maintenance notebook just for the generator.

That evening after dinner, Paul wanted to make the microphone attached to the CB more accessible to him as he drove. At the time, the microphone lay on his left on top of the CB in his peripheral vision area. So Paul stayed in the motorhome while John drove Lib and me on a tour of downtown Salt Lake City.

When we returned to the campground, Paul showed me his completed project. He had fastened a shoelace under the overhead television set and tied it to the microphone so that he had a hanging microphone that would be easy to grasp and use.

The next morning, Tuesday, Day 15, we drove along in 65-degree, luminous weather, hoping to catch a glimpse of the Great Salt Lake. At first it was a blue ribbon in the distance. Finally we saw it close up on our right and pulled into a parking area. Past a single blooming yellow wildflower, over low bushes, beyond the shoreline lay that enormous lake of choppy blue water, extending toward light gray mountains (the Promontory Mountains) almost invisible in the distance, all under wisps of white clouds in a light blue sky.

I-80 is marked as a scenic route along the lake and westward to the Nevada border. We traveled through wide valleys of rangelands. Paul said he wanted to remember to drain the water from the water/fuel separator that evening at the campground. I had a small pad of sticky pages nearby in a pencil holder, so I jotted down his note and stuck it inside the coach on the screen door frame.

Before long we entered northeast Nevada, which a billboard called "Cowboy Country." The interstate on which we traveled is the main street of northern Nevada. It runs more than 400 miles through a dozen communities from the border of Utah to California.

While we did not see any cowboys, we did seen thousands of acres of rangeland as we drove on I-80 that sunlit morning. We also saw 53-foot trailers, double and triple trailers, tankers and double tankers, and car carriers on the level, dual-lane highway, which seemed to invite large trucks and trailers. Sometimes a conversation between truckers came through our CB on channel 17. The usual channel for truckers is 19, but when that gets crowded some truck drivers move to other channels if they just want to talk.

At the end of the day, we were 351 miles closer to California, and we relaxed around the pool and hot tub at the Hi-Desert RV Park in Winnemucca, Nevada. After dinner, Lib and John came by for our departure meeting—to talk over how far we would go the next day and where we would camp. I highlighted on our map with a yellow felt tip pen the next day's route from Winnemucca to Sacramento. We looked in the *Trailer Life Directory* and settled on the Stillman Adult RV Park in Sacramento, the capital of California.

The next day we continued southwest on I-80. After lunch, we rounded a curve and there was a picture postcard city—Reno, with its tall hotels, nestled in a valley with mountains around it.

As we headed toward the California border after passing through Reno, we ascended and descended mountains. Pine trees grew up the sides of the mountains. Sagebrush and dried grass lived compatibly with the pine trees.

All at once we saw a sign: "Welcome to California (Sierra County)." We drove through a narrow valley with the Truckee River glimmering in the sunlight and pine trees pointing skyward everywhere. They refreshed us after driving through the dry plains of Utah and Nevada.

Interstate 80 continued as a dual highway, but our wheels went kathunk, kathunk, kathunk as we drove over patched strips in the concrete surface. We slowed to 50 miles per hour.

We soon entered Tahoe National Forest. Trees along the highway blurred past. We passed signs for Lake Tahoe and Squaw Valley and were stopped at an inspection booth for a gypsy moth inspection. A tall, genial inspector with curly red hair lay down on a creeper to inspect the undersides of both the Graybeals' and our vehicles. In a few minutes, he stood up and announced that we had passed. In addition, he said with a chuckle, neither of our RVs had an oil leak anywhere.

Continuing on I-80 through the Sierra Nevada, we reached Donner Summit, elevation 7,239. I too was on a high—we had arrived in California!

8

Tow Cars and Towables

MANY BOOMERS enjoy using either a travel trailer, fifth wheel, folding camping trailer (known as a pop up), or a truck camper (a hard-sided housekeeping unit loaded onto the back of a pickup truck). These recreational vehicles are also called "towables" because a motorized vehicle such as an automobile or truck tows them.

When motorhomers are new to towing a car, they can think of many reasons not to. Once they've done it, they wonder why they waited. We called our first tow car "Patches" because it had so many rusted places on it that had been patched. It faithfully served us all over the country for 14 years both as a family car and a tow car.

This chapter includes tips on how to drive safely with a tow car or towable and also how to properly set up a towable at your campsite.

Traveling with Towables

❑ Whether you are a seasoned camper or just starting down the road to adventure, when you arrive at your campsite you *must* chock all four wheels both forward and backward. This is especially important to do if you are pulling a trailer, whether it's a 10-foot pop up or a 37-foot fifth wheel, *before* you unhook from the tow vehicle.

—James G. Brown, Finksburg, MD

❏ Follow these easy steps to set up and secure your RV trailer:
  • Position your trailer on the site to your liking.
  • Check to see if you will be able to reach all hookups.
  • Check for trees, tree limbs, or any other objects that would interfere with putting your awning out.
  • Move the trailer forward or backward, whichever is necessary, onto wheel ramps or blocks of wood to level the trailer side to side. (Use a level to check.)
  • Secure trailer wheels with a wheel block front and back so the trailer cannot drift off the ramps.
  • Put a jack base or block of wood under the hitch jack.
  • Turn the hitch jack handle until the trailer is level front to back. (Use a level to check.)
  • Turn the hitch jack handle three turns to lower the front of the trailer. Put a leveling jack flush under each rear corner of the trailer bumper or frame.
  • Turn the hitch jack handle six turns to raise the front of the trailer. Put a leveling jack flush under each front corner of the trailer frame and turn the hitch jack handle three turns to return the trailer to its original position.

Your trailer should now be level and secure. Connect to water, electricity, and sewer, and extend the awning.

—Earl D. Lambert, Westminster, MD

❏ Store a small square of carpet on top of your hitching tools. When you arrive at a site and are ready to unhitch, place the carpet piece on the ground near the hitch. Then you can kneel on it rather than on the ground.

—Connie Burk Davis, Westminster, MD

❑ Here are general tips for using a trailer:

- Check the air pressure in your spare tires.
- Use a checklist before driving away from home or a campsite.
- Do a last walk around the rig, looking under and over for missed details.
- Torque the lug nuts on the wheels.
- Check turn signals and brake, four-way, backup, and running lights every time you hook up the trailer to your vehicle.
- When driving, keep a safe distance behind the vehicle in front. If you can read the license plate of the vehicle in front of you, you are too close.
- Keep to the right when being passed by trucks.
- Don't drive in the blind spot of trucks.
- Be aware of your surroundings. Keep your CB radio and cell phone in good working order. Pay attention to weather conditions.
- Take a break every 100 miles or two hours to keep alert and get circulation.

Be safe, be courteous, be patient, be calm, be friendly, and enjoy!

—William Bucher, Biglerville, PA

❑ Put white lithium grease on the trailer ball. It helps stop squeaking and rust and is a good ground for the wiring.

—Richard Hayden, Leonardtown, MD

Towing a Car

❑ Be sure your tow car is attached safely. While parked on a level place, measure to make sure that the center of the ball on the motorhome hitch is about an inch and a half higher than the pivotal point on the tow bar attached to the car. This keeps the car from pole vaulting into the motorhome during a sudden stop.

❑ If you want to be independent and not inconvenience others when caravaning, tow a car yourself.

❑ When towing a car, allow 100 feet more for braking because you have two vehicles to stop instead of one. Towing a car also affects how closely you should follow another vehicle.

❑ When towing a car, follow the car manufacturer's instructions. Sometimes you must stop at a rest area every 200 or so miles, start the engine, put it in gear in order to circulate the oil, and let it run a while. Also you may have a speed limit for towing your car such as 55 miles per hour. Some newer cars do not have these same limitations—you may drive 65 miles per hour and do not have to start the engine to circulate the oil.

❑ Take a test drive of your motorhome with the tow car attached before your trip. While you're out, use the nearest truck scale to be sure the combined weight of the tow car and the motorhome does not exceed the gross combined vehicle weight (GCVW) recommended by your coach's manufacturer.

❑ To hook up a tow car,
  1. Choose a level spot.
  2. Unfold the tow bar from the front of the tow car.
  3. Lower the socket of the tow bar tongue onto the ball of the hitch at the rear of the motorhome.
  4. Fasten the safety chains between the two vehicles.

5. Connect the tow car's electrical system to the electrical outlet at the rear of the motorhome.

6. Test the electrical connection. Use the turn signals and press down the brake pedal in the motorhome. Both sets of lights should work at the same time.

❑ Towing a car will actually save gas, since you won't be using the motorhome for shorter trips.

❑ Believe it or not, you'll soon forget the tow car is there except when you're passing, parking, stopping quickly, or turning sharply. When passing, make sure both the motorhome and the tow car are completely clear before going back to your lane. When you pull into a rest area or parking lot, allow for the added length of the tow car.

———— ◇ ————

A Short Fork in the Road

WE HAD JUST arrived in California by way of Interstate 80 from the dry Great Basin of Utah and Nevada. While being in California was like finding an oasis in the desert, driving on that stretch of highway was like riding a camel. I wondered how the rough road was affecting the Graybeals since they were towing a car.

When we reached Sacramento, I looked across rooftops and saw my first palm tree in our travels across the country. Shortly afterward, we stopped in front of a black metal sliding gate at the Stillman Adult RV Park. The campground was in the city, where open land was scarce, and so the sites were narrow. Paul skillfully maneuvered the motorhome into our space in a manner that allowed us enough outside area beside a tree to extend the slideout.

That evening the four of us ate in our rigs, then drove to the Florin Mall in the tow car. We easily found the mall from the directions given to us by Maggie in the campground office. Lib and I visited a Regis hair salon and both were pleased with the results. Meanwhile, John and Paul looked around the mall and ate ice cream.

The next morning, Thursday, John took all of us to an Albertson's supermarket. I love to grocery shop when we are away from home. I think it's fun to see what the store carries and talk with the store employees and thus learn a little bit about the people in the area. Paul and I always chat with the cashier also.

John and Lib shopped for groceries, too. We caught up with them at the frozen foods section, our last stop. We checked out simultaneously and were soon stashing our groceries in the Honda station wagon. Coincidentally, each couple spent $60 and confirmed that groceries cost more there than at home.

When we returned to Stillman Park, Paul and I stowed our groceries, some inside the motorhome and some in a basement compartment that we used as a pantry. John and Lib hooked up the tow car to the Southwind and left the park.

I stood outside our motorhome and watched as Paul drove our motorhome out of its site to be sure it did not hit the awnings of the fifth wheel parked only about a foot away from us. We paused for the iron gate to open, drove through, and met up with the Graybeals. It was about 10 o'clock on Day 17 of our trip across the country from Maryland to California.

Leaving Sacramento, we took I-5 south and headed toward Stockton on the first leg of that day's journey. Our destination was the Marina Dunes R.V. Park in Marina, California.

We passed vineyards sparkling with glittery objects meant to scare away birds. We had yet to find a long stretch of smooth road in California. Over the produce farms, fluffy white and gray clouds floated in a powder blue sky. Two big tractor-trailer trucks passed us, their loads of red tomatoes heaped up in open beds. Continuing on I-5, we crossed the California Aqueduct, a wide channel of blue water that flows from northern California to nourish the huge tracts of farmland that need irrigation in the south.

After lunch, we left I-5 for Route 33 and then Route 152 West. From the valley we went into mountains, past the San Luis Reservoir, past a line of whirling windmills on a ridge, and above steep canyons with sharp dropoffs.

From 152 West we turned onto Route 156, a two-lane road. Clouds covered us as we made our way in a rich farming valley toward more mountains. We saw workers hoeing in the fields, farmers burning clumps of vegetation, and orchards. A man sitting on a tractor harrowed a field.

It was almost three o'clock when we passed the welcome sign as we drove up an incline into the Marina Dunes R.V. Park. The campground was clean and well organized. Its price was high—$35 to $40 per night—but it was within walking distance of Monterey Bay.

On that warm, radiant afternoon, John and Paul registered at the office, then backed our motorhomes into sites that were side by side but at slightly different elevations. John and Lib had unhooked the tow car, of course, before backing into their site. The campground was constructed before larger units became popular and therefore was a test of one's driving skills.

While John and Paul and I telephoned people in the area we hoped to visit, Lib cleaned the dust-laden windows of the tow car. A little after five o'clock that evening, the four of us headed a few miles south to Seaside to find a restaurant. Along the main street, Freemont Boulevard, Lib and I spotted one called the Turtle Bay Taqueria.

It turned out that the building contained two restaurants under the same ownership. The Turtle Bay Taqueria featured Mexican food and the Fishwife, which we chose, featured fresh seafood. Some diners sat at tables on the sidewalk in front of the café, apparently enjoying the fresh air and sunshine. Lib and I chose to eat inside since it was too breezy outside for us.

A friendly hostess showed us which tables were available in the dining room and let us choose. Ceramics and paintings decorated the walls. We selected entrées from a large assortment of foods plus the special for the day. Lib ordered a shrimp dish, and the rest of us chose catfish, prepared in a variety of ways.

For dessert, Lib and I ordered key lime pie and John a coconut flan. Paul abstained. The server cleared away our dinner plates, then placed the desserts in front of us and went back for the silverware. I glanced down at the miniature slice of the lime green pie on the small plate in front of me. (Key lime pie always seems to come in tiny slices.)

I was making a note in a small tablet, when I heard our server say, "Here's your fork." Looking up, I saw two forks that looked as long as pitchforks dangling from her hand with the tines facing downward. Lib reached for her fork. I too took one into my hand and paused, looking at the seemingly microscopic piece of pie in front of me on its coin-sized plate.

The server asked, "Is everything all right?"

In my mind, I debated whether I should ask for a shorter fork or just use the long fork. Time was running out. I said, "Yes—I'm fine," but I stayed frozen in time holding the long fork in my left hand.

The server started to leave, then turned and said to me, "Is there anything you would like?" She looked closely at me.

Meanwhile, the others at the table were chuckling and looking at both of us. Finally, I inquired, "Would you have a dessert fork?"

"A dessert fork?" she asked.

"Yes, you know, a *short fork*?" I felt rather foolish asking this when I didn't know what their supply of silverware included.

"No, we don't have that." She thought quickly. "Would you like a cocktail fork?" she offered.

Rather embarrassed by the whole conversation, I said, "No, that's okay. This will be fine."

I sheepishly switched the long fork to my right hand to begin eating. Still laughing, the others agreed that the forks in that restaurant had extra long handles. The more I thought about using a cocktail fork to eat my pie and holding the long fork while hoping for a short one, the more the laughter welled up within me, too. We had found both a good restaurant and a source of hilarity that would last the rest of our trip.

The next day was "Rendevous Day" for the Alaskan caravaners. I hand vacuumed the carpet and scatter rugs, swept the ceramic-tiled floors, dusted the windows and leather lounge, washed the bathroom basin, and otherwise cleaned and straightened up the motorhome. Paul set up the new satellite dish outside on a picnic table. He made sure there was a clear line of sight between the dish and the satellite with practically no obstructions such as trees between the two.

Paul said he was glad he did not have to drive anywhere the next day. We had been on the road 17 days, most of which were long travel days. Our odometer clocked 3,648 miles.

Unlike the first three reunions of our group in Maryland, Montana, and Louisiana, when nine of the 10 couples and our tailgunner attended, this time only six couples were signed up. In addition to our hosts, the Swagertys, who lived in California, Mary Jo and Bill Cornell from Connecticut, Jackie and Lyle Wrigley from Michigan and Florida, Yvonne and Wil Foreman from Louisiana, and we two couples from Maryland planned to attend. Mary Jo and Bill had sold their motorhome and planned to fly to California and rent a cabin at the two campgrounds where we'd be staying.

After a trip to Santa Cruz to visit a friend of the Graybeals, we drove straight back to the campground, where we found the Wrigleys had parked their Holiday Rambler motorhome next to ours on the uphill side.

Lyle Wrigley was washing his white Saturn tow car. He had a tale to tell about their trip West—high winds on I-80 tipped over another motorhome and oil leaked from his air conditioner, splattering his tow car.

Lyle told us that Mary Jo and Bill Cornell arrived driving the Swagertys' motorhome and then had gone for propane. Lyle's wife, Jackie, was at the campground office. The unbelievable news was that Effie and Clem Swagerty would not be coming because Clem was in the hospital.

Soon the Cornells returned to the campground in the Swagertys' Cross Country motorhome and parked in the site uphill from the Wrigleys. Our group was lined up together—Graybeals, Beards, Wrigleys, and Cornells at the top.

We all went to greet Bill and Mary Jo with hugs and kisses. As Mary Jo put away groceries, she told us that they had arrived at the Swagertys on Thursday to find that Clem was in the hospital. Effie had expected him to come home the day before, but Clem's condition worsened—his kidneys were shutting down. It seems that medicine given to Clem was causing problems.

So Bill drove the Swagertys' motorhome to the campground— the first time he had driven a Type A motorhome. He was not thrilled about the responsibility of driving someone else's vehicle.

We learned also from Mary Jo that the Foremans were not coming either. That meant only four couples would attend the reunion. We were on our own with a link by telephone with Effie and a bagful of sightseeing materials she had gathered. Mary Jo said that Effie had planned to host our first evening meal to-gether in the park's club room, but of course that could not be.

We were all in a state of uncertainty. We were used to having a "wagonmaster"—a role played by the host—who made the advance arrangements and guided us day by day. Clem and Effie had made reservations for our group at two campgrounds—one south of San Francisco and one north. Effie had planned to share the destination brochures with us and recommend sights for us to see.

That changed suddenly with Clem's health problems. When he became ill, it was too late for Effie to change the reservations without forfeiting the deposits. In addition, the Graybeals, the Wrigleys, and we were already on our way to California. When Yvonne Foreman in Louisiana talked with Effie and learned about Clem's health, she decided that she and Wil would not attend and would instead visit relatives.

Mary Jo said she wanted to fix her famous chicken breast entrée for our first dinner together. Realizing that with the slide-out, our coach had ample room for the entire group, I offered our rig for the evening meal.

And so, rising to the occasion, we planned who would bring what. Soon Mary Jo was preparing her entrée. The rest of us pitched in in whatever way we could.

Paul set up the Graybeals' card table in the living room area and put in the leaf for our dinette table. We could easily accommodate eight diners.

While all of this was going on, Jackie came by our motorhome to invite us to their motorhome at five o'clock for hors d'oeuvres. She said to bring our own drinks.

As the eight of us sat in the Wrigleys' motorhome, which also had a slideout, Mary Jo went through some of Effie's notes and the sightseeing materials she had collected. Not knowing the area or what the Swagertys would recommend, we blindly decided to try to see the Monterey Bay Aquarium the next day. I was to call in the morning to make reservations.

Our group then flowed down the hillside to our coach for dinner. We had a great time eating and talking. We all laughed about my "short fork" incident the day before at the Seaside restaurant.

I wanted to figure out exactly what we would do the next day, so I asked John to help with route planning, something at which he was an ace. We decided to go in cars—the Wrigleys' and the Graybeals', and to leave at 10 o'clock.

As the party broke up, each couple took their leftover food and drink back to their motorhome. Paul and I cleaned our dishes and straightened up the coach. Then we walked to the office to use the telephone to call Effie. We ran into Mary Jo, who had just finished talking with her. Clem's condition had not improved.

I dialed Effie's number. It was so good to hear her voice, although it contained concern for Clem. She said her family was there to support her. She was glad we were having a good time and wished us well, saying that she would be with us in spirit. I told her she and Clem would be in our thoughts and asked her to give Clem our love.

Paul and I walked back to the rig, our steps heavy with the news about Clem. By 10 o'clock, Paul was in bed and I was writing in my journal. I tried to assess our situation. We were all glad to be together again but a bit unsettled by the turn of events. All we could do was pray. I wrote a prayer in my journal and then turned off the computer, silently wishing Clem a speedy recovery.

9

Destinations and Sightseeing

GENEALOGY, ROCK hounding, race cars, nature, sightseeing—every RVer has a passion for something that takes him or her on the road. The destinations are many. Here are some terrific suggestions that will make pursuing your passions more pleasurable.

❑ Motorhoming genealogists know that their mobility affords them unique opportunities for family tree research. They can plan trips to research areas, taking photos of ancestral homesteads and church sites and cemetery tombstones, and gather "obits" and other pieces of family history from the pages of local newspapers. Contact local genealogical societies in your area and let them know your routes and destinations. You may find members, unable to travel themselves, who will pay you to act as a researcher/ photographer for *their* family tree needs. Plan your trips so you arrive on a day when civic offices are open—not weekends.
—Bruce Allsen, Moreno Valley, CA

❑ Before photographing an old gravestone, wet it with water so the lettering will show up better.

❑ When planning a trip, leave some free time to see whatever museums or other places that interest you as you go along.

❑ Be alert for unusual wildlife, flowers, and scenic beauty. Enjoy nature—touch it, feel it, smell it, listen to it, and look at it.

❑ To see the Grand Tetons at their best on the eastern side, approach them from the north.

❑ The most dramatic way to see Sedona and the red rocks is to approach from the north. (From Flagstaff, take Exit 337 off I-17, turn left at the stop sign, and follow the signs to Route 89A. Turn left again to Sedona on 89A South. Travel 23 miles to Sedona on a two-lane, paved road through a forest of mostly pine trees. Descend a winding road along mountain rocky walls.)

❑ Check road maps for upcoming rest areas or picnic areas and welcome centers. (You may not think you want information at a welcome center as you approach it, but experience tells me that every time I pass one by, I later wish I had stopped either for a map of that state or for general information that would help me identify what I was seeing.)

❑ Pay close attention to the directions to your campground and orient yourself using a map. You may need to know later how to go into town and back.

❑ The Grand Balloon Ascension near Tucson, Arizona, is known as one of the 10 best hot-air balloon events in the nation. It's worth a special trip.

❑ When you're heading for higher elevations, watch out for altitude sickness. Allow extra time to acclimate yourself to the thinner air. It's a good idea to stay at 5,000 feet for a day or two before going higher. At 5,000 feet, it's normal to notice a faster heartbeat and increased breathing rate due to lower oxygen levels. For the first two or three days, some people may experience dizziness, fatigue, headaches, nasal congestion, and difficulty sleeping. If the altitude starts to bother you, take deep breaths; avoid overexertion; eat high-carbohydrate foods; go easy on alcohol, caffeine, and salty foods; and drink more water than usual.

❑ You'll take more pictures if your camera is handy. Keep it beside the passenger seat and have a purse or fanny pack that's big enough to hold it.

❑ If you'd like to travel to a remote location such as Alaska but are not sure you can handle it on your own, consider an RV caravan. Touring by caravan has a lot of advantages. The sponsoring group plans the itinerary and makes advance reservations for campgrounds and group activities such as meals, ferries, sightseeing, and shows.

———————— ◇ ————————

Exploring on Our Own

IN THE ABSENCE of our hosts, we had decided to see the Monterey Bay Aquarium and Cannery Row on Saturday, visit the National Steinbeck Center followed by the 17-Mile Drive on Sunday, and take the Roaring Camp & Big Trees Narrow-Gauge

Railroad train ride into the redwoods on Monday. None of us had ever been to those places, but they all sounded interesting.

With no official wagonmaster, Mary Jo and Bill fell into the role by virtue of having arrived in the hosts' motorhome. I tried to help Mary Jo by doing some of the telephoning for information and reservations. She told me she needed a sidekick and I was glad to oblige.

John took on the role of navigator with Paul's help since John drove the tow car and Paul sat in front with a road map while Lib and I sat in back. The Wrigleys and Cornells preferred to follow in the Wrigleys' tow car. Since our cars did not have CBs through which we could talk back and forth as we traveled on the road, Bill and Paul each held one of the two-way communicators to use for that purpose.

On Saturday morning, we left the campground in the two tow cars and took Route 1 to Monterey. We soon stood outside in a fast-moving line for tickets to the aquarium. It was a clear day with a cool breeze but warm in the sunshine. A large modern building complex located on the rocky edge of Monterey Bay, the aquarium exhibits the flora and fauna of the bay. Inside the busy, noisy, cavernous lobby we joined hundreds of other visitors, many of them families with toddlers in strollers and young children.

Using a visitor map, we began to explore. We saw the Kelp Forest exhibit through the largest window on Earth, a million-gallon indoor replication of the ocean with fish weaving in and out among the underwater plants. Children enjoyed interactive touch pools where they could actually handle a sea star or touch a harmless bat ray. Various windows let us see unique marine life in their habitats from large sharks to tiny sardines. The graceful pulsing and drifting of beautiful jellyfish fascinated me. The highlight for me was the exhibit of black-footed penguins in the "Splash Zone" gallery. For some reason, penquins bring out a mirthful feeling in me. Maybe it's because they look and act so formal.

After completing our visit to the aquarium, we four women browsed and shopped in the nearby Cannery Row, made famous by John Steinbeck in his book by the same name, published in 1945. Our spouses sat on a sidewalk bench, taking in the environment.

Mary Jo and Bill scouted the area for a restaurant and chose the Cannery Grill. Everyone enjoyed the food. The ice cream lovers in our group were disappointed, however, because that treat was not available on the menu. So the Wrigleys invited us all to their rig for an ice cream social that evening.

About six o'clock that evening, Effie called me with the good news that Clem was much better. She couldn't believe how he had improved. She revealed that the doctor hadn't expected him to live through the night. A sense of relief rushed through me.

I took the good news about Clem to the Wrigleys' social hour. As we ate our ice cream, we talked, laughed, and had fun together.

A little after noon on Sunday, we left the RV park in the tow cars and headed toward Salinas and the National Steinbeck Center, a half-hour's drive away. After we parked, we had lunch in the center's café and then bought admission tickets in the museum store. As I walked into the enormous, high-ceilinged lobby of the center to tour the exhibits, I caught my breath. I felt a special awe to be in the presence of so much of John Steinbeck. I had read and studied his *Grapes of Wrath* in American Literature in college.

I wandered among many interactive exhibits—pulled open drawers that were lighted and covered with acrylic and that housed letters and other memorabilia, listened on an old-fashioned telephone to a reading of part of a Steinbeck novel, watched a video scene of a Steinbeck movie, and listened to Steinbeck giving his speech when accepting the Nobel Prize for literature. There was so much to see, I almost missed the truck camper, Rocinante, in which Steinbeck and his dog Charley toured the United States, a trip that was the basis for his *Travels with Charley.*

About four o'clock we left the center. From Salinas we took Route 68 and then Route 1 to reach the famous 17-Mile Drive along the southwestern Monterey Peninsula. At a toll gate, we paid $7.75 for each car.

We entered a tree-lined, paved, two-lane road; a broken red line painted between the two yellow center lines identified the scenic drive. Using Effie's brochures to guide us, we began a series of stops at breathtaking viewpoints along the drive. At Spanish Bay, Paul took off his shoes and let the bay water lick his ankles; at Point Joe, Lyle and the rest of us looked out at the Restless Sea and at the California coastline stretching toward Big Sur.

The most beautiful stop was the Pebble Beach Golf Links. We walked through the lobby of the lodge and onto the balcony. The much-televised 18th green with the familiar wind-sculpted cypress tree and the Monterey Bay lay peacefully before us. The greens looked smooth, healthy, and well watered. The rocky top of a distant mountain across the bay was highlighted by the setting sun.

We returned to the campground about 6:45 that day. John arranged another ice cream social in the Wrigleys' unit. As a joke, Jackie presented me with a pickle fork to use to eat my dessert. After an enjoyable hour, Paul and I returned to our motorhome.

As I was preparing to write in my laptop, the cell phone rang. It was Effie. Clem was much better, she reported, but she did not know when he could go home. She and I went over plans for Monday's trip to Roaring Camp & Big Trees Narrow-Gauge Railroad. She advised us to make reservations.

On Monday morning, Mary Jo and I walked down the hill to the pay phones at the campground office. She called Roaring Camp and learned that the train ride was one hour in each direction up and down Bear Mountain. Parking was available for rigs as large as 40 feet long. There was only one departure weekdays at 11:00 A.M. at that time of year.

Since the drive north from Marina to Felton, where we would catch the train, would take one and a half hours, our tow car caravan left the campground at 8:56. We were glad that we left in good time because as we went north on Route 1, we had to detour due to road construction. The communicators helped us keep in touch during the detour and intervening traffic. We arrived at our destination with time to spare.

Roaring Camp contained the railroad station and a general store, where we bought our tickets, and several other buildings. No train was in sight. A few moments later, a steam engine pulling several yellow and black open cars and a caboose with a roof and open windows stopped on the track beside the station. The engine itself stood beside a water tower, where the engineer put water into the boiler.

The conductor shouted, "All aboard!" We hurried to the second open car behind the engine. We sat on a long bench fastened to the sides of the open car, riding sideways. Each car held about 30 people.

Promptly at 11:00, the conductor announced over the loudspeaker that passengers were not to stand up, smoke, or hang their arms out and grab trees, which might be poison oak. The whistle blew. The bell rang. Our car started with a jerk.

The conductor came by to collect tickets, then returned to the caboose and began to give the history of the railroad and the area. A pleasant and knowledgeable guide, he told us his name was John, that he was 71 years old, and that he worked three days a week as the conductor on the train.

Soon we entered the Redwood Forest on Bear Mountain.

We rode over a trestle that was 210 feet long and into the tightest curved track in the United States. Past the trestle, the conductor pointed out a fallen redwood log that was 1,140 years old, according to its counted rings.

The redwoods were so tall that I could not bend my head back far enough to see their tops. One standing tree was 325 feet high and 1,500 years old. Deciduous trees and green beeches lived among the redwoods. Feathery ferns, poison oak, and fine green moss grew closer to the forest floor.

Most of us got off the train for a short stop on the mountain to visit a sanctuary of trees called Cathedral Grove. It was a natural arena surrounded by fog or coastal redwoods that are 600–700 years old.

Conductor John stood on a huge flat stump as train riders clustered below him. As he talked, I walked over to a nearby redwood and touched gently its rough bark. Then I looked skyward. A circle of tree trunks and branches converged toward a small orb of sky as if the opening were the light at the end of an evergreen tunnel.

After lunch in Felton, we drove back to the campground at a leisurely pace, soaking in the scenery. Tomorrow we would be leaving the Monterey Bay area.

10

Renting or Buying an RV and Adapting the Interior of Your Rig

No MATTER how long you've owned an RV, you're probably always looking for ways to make the interior more livable. Whether you're an RV renter or owner, you'll find tips here that will help you get greater enjoyment from your next trip.

Renting an RV

❑ When you rent an RV, make sure you fully understand how everything works. (Before our customers leave with their RVs, we do a walk around and walk through.) You should know how to use the stove, toilet, and shower, what to do when the pilot light on the water heater goes out, how to read the gauges, and how to dump.

—Paul LeClair, Bates Motor Home Rentals of Rapid City, Black Hawk, SD

❑ In this area (where there are 2,000 campsites nearby), a lot of people don't want to own a travel trailer but prefer to rent one. That way, they don't have to worry about storage or maintenance. I don't let customers leave until I go over the travel trailer from front to rear—awning, microwave, stereo, VCR, every inch—even if they are in a hurry.

—Carl Rochelle, Diamond Lakes RV Rentals and Sales Co., Hot Springs, AR

Purchasing an RV

❑ Carefully consider all your needs before buying an RV. The most common mistake is buying a unit that's too small. Young customers with growing families should consider the resale value of an RV. Items such as bunk beds and booths that convert into beds are great for young families or for couples who want to take their grand-children camping with them. If you like to take your pets when you travel, remember that linoleum or vinyl flooring is easier to keep clean than carpeting. For dry camping without an auxiliary generator to provide electricity, many people here in Wyoming purchase 15-watt solar panels, mount them on the roof of their trailer, and use them to keep extra batteries charged.

—Jean Stahla, Eastside Motors & RV's, Inc., Gillette, WY

❑ Consider renting an RV before buying so that you know what you really want. If you purchase an RV from a dealer who also rents, see if a credit for the rental can be applied toward the purchase of the RV.

—Paul LeClair, Black Hills RV, Black Hawk, SD

❑ If you plan to purchase an RV, talk with other people who have purchased RVs and find out if they were happy with their dealer. Our job as a dealer is to find customers the best built camper for the dollar. Every once in a while a customer gets a camper with problems that they will want the dealer to take care of; therefore, it is important to buy from a dealer recommended by others.

—Jane Bauder, Sterling RV Center, Sterling, CO

Adapting the Interior

❑ For hidden storage for valuables or for canned goods, pull out the bottom drawer of cabinets. There is always dead space between the floor and the drawer bottom—usually nicely padded with carpet.

—Mary Jo Cornell, Fairfield, CT

❑ The space over the side door of some RVs is great for a bookshelf. Hold the shelf up with angle brackets, put cup hooks at each end between cabinets, and attach bungee cords between the hooks to hold the books on the shelf when traveling. If you have upholstery above the door opening, remove it and tack it to the underside of the shelf. Be sure the shelf is high enough to clear your head when you climb the steps to enter the RV.

—Mary Jo and Bill Cornell, Fairfield, CT

❑ When we wanted to replace privacy curtains in our Type C motorhome, we found some inexpensive, well-made, multipocketed fabric panels, each about half the width of an average shower curtain, with grommets on top. We hung the panels on the track that's just behind the front seats of the motorhome. The track already had little hooks in it, so we matched the panel grommets with the hooks. When closed, the panels "isolate" the cab area above the front seats from the main area of the RV. The pockets come in many sizes and are closed by a variety of means: Velcro, belts, zippers, ties, snaps, etc., which provide visual interest and are lots of fun for our grand-daughters. Both of them have selected special pockets for storage of toys and for items that they find during the trip. For the adults, some much-appreciated additional stowing places make these panels a worthwhile purchase.

—Joan B. Peterson, Ph.D., Madison, Wisconsin

❑ A quick, easy, and inexpensive way to keep cabinets from opening while moving is to use elastic ponytail clasps (the kind with two balls on the ends of the elastic band). Where two cabinet door handles are placed next to each other, run the elastic portion of the clasp through the handles and then secure the clasp with the decorative balls. These little elastic ponytail clasps do the trick and are amazingly strong and cheap. (Go to the dollar store and buy them by the bag!)

—Ed Holm, Millsboro, DE

❑ Use carpet on the shelves of cupboards. It cuts down on noise and decreases vibration that could cause breakage. Carpet samples or remnants can be obtained at carpet stores inexpensively or sometimes for free. Use a razor blade knife or a carpet cutter to cut pieces to fit the shelves. Heavy scissors such as tin shears are also useful for cutting.

—Joyce and Carroll Dell, Littlestown, PA

❑ To keep dishes from rattling, store them in bags made from quilted fabric or put quilted material between them.

—Elizabeth Graybeal, Hampstead, MD

❑ Insert clear acrylic strips at the front of shelves in the medicine cabinet or other cupboards that hold small items. The clear strips will keep items from falling forward when you open the cupboard door, and you can easily see what's behind the strips. You can buy the strips at a local lumber yard, where someone there will cut them to the size that you need. Measure the width of the space plus the framing behind which you will place the acrylic strip. Decide on what height you want the strip to be. Have these measurements with you when you go to the lumber yard.

❑ A small clock affixed to the dash will help you keep track of the time as you drive. A thermometer attached to the driver's side mirror also provides useful information.

❑ Use strips of self-adhesive hook-and-loop fastener (such as Velcro) to hang small framed pictures to the walls of your RV. Stick pieces of the fastener to the back of the picture frame, either on all four corners or along the top and bottom, and corresponding pieces to the wall. To hang the picture, press the fasteners on the picture frame onto the fasteners adhered to the wall until the frame is secure.

❑ A strip of hook-and-loop fastener will keep draperies tightly closed where they meet in the center of the window. Sew one side of the strip to the front of the leading edge of one drapery panel and the other side of the strip to the back of the corresponding panel. Press together, of course, to keep the draperies closed.

❑ In a motorhome, usually a drapery hangs over a large part of the side passenger window. When driving past beautiful scenery, gather the drapery beside or around the adjacent vertical handle bar. Then wrap a short bungee cord around both the drapery and the bar. You may want to secure the drapery at a second place on the bar with a second bungee cord. Bungee cords are available in various sizes at many RV dealer accessory stores, camping stores, campground stores, and hardware stores.

❑ Having a tiled shower/tub means it must be wiped down after each use. Keep a towel handy on the retractable clothesline above the tub, if available, for this duty.

❑ Keep the following items in the RV: baking soda, sugar, salt, laundry and dishwashing supplies, first-aid supplies, bathroom tissue, paper towels, plastic utensils, trash bags, paper plates, cups, napkins, bed linens, umbrella, galoshes, rain gear, and mechanic's overalls.

—————— ◇ ——————

On to Petaluma

AFTER RETURNING FROM the Roaring Camp & Big Trees Narrow-Gauge Railroad train ride, we assembled that Monday evening at Mary Jo Cornell's suggestion for a departure meeting in the game room of the Marina Dunes R.V. Park.

Gathered around a coffee table, we planned our route from Marina north to Walnut Creek and northwest to Petaluma for the next day. Bill and Mary Jo had decided to return the Swagertys' motorhome the next day when we visited Effie at Walnut Creek. The Cornells did not know whether they would rent a cabin or stay in a motel or hotel in Petaluma, our next camping site. They did know that driving someone else's motorhome was a burden to them. I'm sure the Swagertys had modified the RV to suit their own needs, but the Cornells were unfamiliar with the rig and were afraid something might go wrong while they were using it.

After the meeting, Mary Jo and Bill cleaned out the borrowed motorhome to prepare to return it the next day. They stowed their goods in the tow car of the Wrigleys, with whom they planned to ride from Walnut Creek to Petaluma. Mary Jo said she had put her groceries in the bathtub instead of cupboards so that when they turned in the rig, it would be easy to retrieve the groceries.

On Tuesday morning, we left Marina Dunes R.V. Park. I glanced at my watch; it was 8:44. We had found the park's office staff accommodating and friendly.

Arriving at Walnut Creek, we parked our four motorhomes and tow cars in the parking lot of the Presbyterian church to which Clem and Effie belong. Effie had permission from her pastor for us to park there while we visited her.

The Cornells and Wrigleys had arrived ahead of us and were waiting. The pastor happened to be in the lot when we arrived. He kindly took three of us in his car, and the other four went in John's car. As a result, the Wrigleys did not have to unhook their tow car. I called Effie on our cell phone to let her know that we were at the parking lot and would be seeing her soon.

Effie's wide smile and twinkling eyes welcomed us. She told me that the stress of the last few months had caused her to lose weight, but she felt fine.

We walked across the parking area to the condominium that she and Clem have shared for many years. What a lovely surprise we found! The dining room table was set with elegance—lace tablecloth, china dinnerware, and silver service that included a *short* fork!

As we ate, Effie worked from printed materials in her lap and went over the possibilities of what to see and do in the San Francisco area. In her gentle voice, she gave us directions to the campground at Petaluma and said she thought we would like it. She and Clem had camped there several times.

After a phone call to Clem and hugs for Effie, our three-motorhome caravan left Walnut Creek heading north to Petaluma, California. We led with the Wrigleys and the Graybeals following in that order. Mary Jo and Bill had left the Swagertys' motorhome in the church parking lot with great relief.

We skirted the large San Pablo Bay on its north rim and crossed the Petaluma River. Paul commented that the new location of the CB microphone made it much easier to use. After a two-hour drive, we turned into a beautifully landscaped entrance on a smooth asphalted road and drove past a small meadow with goats, ducks, and geese on our right. Shortly, we parked at the office of the San Francisco North/Petaluma KOA Kampground.

Our site, as did most of the other sites at the campground, had a shade tree and ample room for the slideout. I looked out the front windows of the motorhome as I sat at my desk area. The leaves of short and tall shade trees moved gently in the breeze. Sunlight brightened picnic tables at the sites. We had survived all of the uncertainties that awaited us at the first campground. After being with Effie at lunch and hearing what she had in mind for us, I felt more secure about our time at Petaluma.

Mary Jo reserved the recreation room for a five o'clock meeting for the eight of us, and the campground left it unlocked for us. John brought to the meeting the *Petaluma Visitors Guide,* a supplement of the *Petaluma Argus-Courier* furnished by the campground, which showed maps and what to do in the area. When we registered, each couple had paid for a tour of San Francisco for Friday. We discussed what to do during the intervening Wednesday and Thursday. The Wrigleys and Graybeals wanted to reserve a tee time for golf. They would use the Graybeals' station wagon since it could hold four sets of golf clubs plus four passengers. The Graybeals also talked about taking a tour of the area the next morning, something everyone wanted to do.

During the meeting, Mary Jo said that she wanted to heat soup on the stove in the recreation room and asked if someone would lend her a pan. Both Lib and Jackie volunteered the equipment. The cabin that she and Bill were renting had no cooking facilities.

After the meeting, Paul and I came back to our motorhome to fix frozen meals for ourselves. I couldn't really enjoy eating a delicious, well-balanced dinner when I knew Mary Jo and Bill were making do with soup. So I walked to the Cornells' cabin and invited them to join us for frozen entrées.

When the Cornells arrived, Mary Jo had three eggs that she wanted to hard boil. They were left over from camping in the Swagertys' motorhome at Marina Dunes, and she wanted to cook them before they spoiled.

She had no idea, of course, that I had the odd notion of never using the burners on my stove. We had our first motorhome for 12 years and I never used the stovetop burners except to turn them on to be sure they worked when we first got the rig. Not only that, but I had never used the new saucepan that was perfect for boiling the three eggs. Its cellophane wrapper was unbroken.

"You never use them? Why not? Don't they work?" Mary Jo's jaw had dropped.

"Well, I just never wanted to clean them up afterward," I said lamely. "But I'm going to christen them now. I'm even going to try out a new pan." I personally placed the pan containing the eggs over the circle of flames.

As I set the table, I kept an eye on the eggs. I reached above the dining table into overhead cabinets for the Corningware plates stored there. It was easy to retrieve them because Paul had made removable wooden shelves on short legs for three of the cabinets. On the shelves, I could place stacks of dishes of the same size—dinner, bread and butter, cereal bowls, and others—without having to lift one size off another in order to use what was underneath.

I got individual servings of applesauce from the can cupboard above the toilet. The toilet area came with an overhead cupboard in which we stored towels, bath tissue, and deodorizer. In the space beneath it, Paul hung a wood cupboard with adjustable shelves. Its depth was just right for canned goods. He matched the paneling of the two can cupboard doors with that of the overhead doors above. We laughingly refer to this cupboard as the can cupboard in the can!

The Cornells had not eaten commercially frozen meals before and said they surprisingly enjoyed them. After dinner, they left in the dark carrying their hard-boiled eggs cooked on a virgin stovetop.

Thankfully, the stove burners required no cleaning. Smiling, I congratulated them on their spill-free premiere and gently unfolded the cover over them until the next exigency.

Paul helped straighten up the interior of the rig. He slid trash through a tilt down door and into a large wooden wastebasket with a plastic liner bag. One of the first projects that Paul undertook in our new motorhome was to make two wastebaskets— one for the kitchen and one for the bathroom. He had converted a large cupboard space under the sink that originally came equipped with a pullout, wire-framed compartment for storing tall items. Just above the door to the cupboard was a tilt-down spice rack. When Paul removed the spice rack, it was possible to slide items through the tilt-down door into the space below. Paul removed the wire rack and the tracks from the bottom cupboard and set inside a large wooden wastebasket he made. With the tilt-down door, we don't have to open and close the large door every time we want to put something into the wastebasket.

In the bathroom, Paul made another wood container that fit under the left side of the sink top and spanned the narrow distance between the sink and the shower wall. He padded the sides with heavy flannel to protect the shower wall and the cabinet wall. We were surprised at how much trash that odd-sized basket held.

It was almost eleven o'clock on the next morning, Wednesday, when we left the Petaluma KOA in our two tow cars, driven by John and Lyle, to sightsee in the area. We entered the city of

Napa and made our way to the public parking garage of the Tourist Information and Visitor Center. A hospitable woman at the visitor center seemed disappointed that we wanted to visit only one winery, but she cheerfully gave us information and a map and suggested several places to eat lunch in the immediate area.

We drove to Domaine Chandon, Yountville, in Napa Valley. Under the warm California sun, we walked across a footbridge through beautifully landscaped grounds to the entrance of the winery. In the wine shop/gift shop, we learned that the next tour would occur in about 30 minutes, at 3 P.M. Meanwhile, we browsed in the gift shop and wandered around the large gallery, looking at displays.

Our tour guide, Larry, met us in the gallery. He led us up concrete steps to the atrium area, where we sat on more concrete steps while Larry entertained us with the story of how sparkling wine is made as well as the history of Domaine Chandon.

Then he took us inside the winery itself, where we saw enormous shiny drums containing wines of various vintages (years when they were made). He explained the very fine art of the winemaker, the one who actually tastes the wine and decides what needs to be added so the wine can be depended upon to taste the same from year to year.

Next, we saw the bottling and wrapping process. I was impressed with how clean the environment was all along the route in the enormous warehouse-style building. We passed on the invitation to taste the wine and headed back to the campground by scenic route Oakville Grade. It wound through hills and canyons with very little traffic and very few buildings.

Midmorning the next day, Thursday, the Graybeals and Wrigleys set off in the Graybeals' car for a nearby golf course. That morning Paul and I did odds and ends. At noon, Bill drove the Wrigleys' car with Mary Jo, Paul, and me into Petaluma for lunch.

I was looking forward to Friday and our tour of San Francisco. The bright, colorful brochure from the campground described our tour. If scheduling permitted, passengers might leave the tour vehicle for "a close-up look" at the Golden Gate Bridge. Long views of the graceful span are picturesque, but actually walking on it would be exciting. The brochure promised "a wonderful day in the city."

At eight o'clock on a cool, foggy, Friday morning, 13 people from the campground boarded a white passenger van lettered outside with "Petaluma KOA." Driver and tour guide Donna Piezzi soon headed for San Francisco, 39 miles south. On the way, in answer to our questions, she said that California was not having a drought, but the dry conditions were normal for late September until the rainy season started. She told the history of Petaluma, saying that gold was discovered at Sutter's Mill near Petaluma at Sacramento. The Petaluma area contains chicken ranches and other kinds of ranches.

As we drew nearer to the Golden Gate Bridge and then drove on it, Donna told us that it opened in 1937. Although it is called "golden," its official color is "international orange." The bridge is named for the narrow strait of water it spans, called the Golden Gate, between the Pacific Ocean and San Francisco Bay. It joins Marin County with San Francisco. Over 100,000 cars use it daily.

Just past the bridge, our driver headed the van into the visitors center parking area. Before I knew it, my feet were walking on the wide sidewalk of the world-famous Golden Gate Bridge. Traffic whizzed past in the six lanes to my left, vibrating the bridge. To my surprise, the bridge curved ahead. In the cool morning air, I paused beside the four-foot-high, international orange metal railing. Far below was the shoreline of the San Francisco Bay, its blue water turning to whitecaps against rocks that looked like pebbles. Parked cars became tiny miniatures. I saw the top of what looked like a fort with an open curved bastion that faced the bay. In the distant fog, Alcatraz Island loomed on the horizon like a great gray battleship.

Soon we rode into Golden Gate Park—once sand dunes but now an 1,100-acre verdant garden, the largest man-made park in the world. Our driver parked near the Japanese Tea Garden. It was a foggy 40 degrees in the park. Paul did not go, but I entered the Japanese Tea Garden. Admission was $1.25. I wandered peacefully among the bonsai and other exotic plants, walked over arched bridges, watched goldfish swimming in small ponds, stepped on smooth stones, and felt awe at a multistoried pagoda. It was almost time to return to the van, but I sipped tea in the Japanese Tea House served by a young kimono-clad woman.

By the time we arrived at the cable car stop, the sun had come out. Donna told us that the cable cars were the only moving national monument in the United States. A cable car made its first run up Nob Hill on August 1, 1873. Today, about 37 cars run on 17 miles of track in the city.

We boarded, sat on seats facing one another, held onto a pole nearby, heard the familiar clang clang of the bell, and then began a memorable 15-minute ride by cable car. I had no idea the hills of San Francisco were so steep! A gripman and a conductor operated the car. I talked with the tall, muscular gripman, who told me that he started or stopped the car by operating the grip that grasped or released the moving cable. The continuously running cable lay below street level.

Our next stop was Fisherman's Wharf, busy with tourists and vendors and the source of fresh seafood, primarily Dungeness crab, shrimp, abalone, squid, sea bass, mackerel, salmon, and cod. Far across the water, I saw Alcatraz Island, now in sunlight. A former federal penitentiary, it is now part of the National Park system. Tour boats leave from Pier 41 to take visitors to the island. I walked past Pier 41; a visit to Alcatraz was not on our schedule that day.

From the wharf we rode to Chinatown. With yellow banners and red printing in both Chinese and English strung high across the street, the area seemed festive. Nearly 80,000 Chinese-Americans, or about one-tenth of San Francisco's population, live in Chinatown. Shops line the streets offering old ivory, jade, teak, and other treasures as well as fresh produce.

During our tour of San Francisco, Donna pointed out many landmarks such as Lombard Street, "The Crookedest Street in the World," which zigzags sharply down a steep hill. Our final stop was Fort Point, beneath the Golden Gate Bridge, whose roof I had seen from the bridge that morning.

I stood in the parking lot at Fort Point and looked up at the awesome concrete pillars and intricate yet mighty metal framework supporting the bridge. I felt a sense of appreciation for the designer and builders of that magnificent structure. I looked across the bay where it curved inland. The skyline of San Francisco faced me.

We arrived back at the San Francisco North/Petaluma KOA Kampground about 4:30 as scheduled, thankful for Donna, her excellent driving skills, friendly manner, and information. She had fulfilled the promises of the bright travel brochure—I had walked on the Golden Gate Bridge and had indeed had "a wonderful day in the city."

11

Driving, Mileage, and Fuel

BASIC TO any RVing trip is, of course, driving and maintaining either the vehicle that pulls the towable or a motorhome. RVers are always learning better and more ways to do things. In this chapter, experienced RVers share tips that make driving safer and more fuel-efficient.

Driving and Mileage

❑ If semi trucks seem to blow you off the road when they pass you, Camping World sells a product called Steer Safe Stabilizer. It really helps also on soft shoulders.

—Louis and Ann Beeler, Salome, AZ

❑ For those who need to limit the amount of fluids or caffeine they drink when traveling, freeze a small bottle of water, then put it in an insulated cup holder. You can sip from it all day as you drive.

—Robert Witter, Westminster, MD

❑ As you approach a line of barrels in road construction areas, watch out for any that are protruding into your lane.

❑ Be alert to possible overhead obstructions. You'll avoid having a tree limb, low gas station roof, or low overpass tear off your antenna or rooftop air conditioner or scratch or dent the exterior of your RV.

❑ Avoid driving downtown through a large city unless the interstate takes you through it. There is often construction, many traffic lights, and much traffic.

❑ Share the driving if possible. Even drivers who say they like to drive appreciate a respite from a full day behind the wheel. Every driver in the family should practice and become comfortable driving the RV before the trip.

❑ Keep your gas tank at least one-fourth full at all times. If you're in an area where gasoline stations are few and far between, try to keep the tank more than half full.

❑ To get better mileage, (1) avoid driving with the water tank full (a gallon of water weighs about 8.2 pounds), and (2) drive at 55 miles per hour for gasoline engines or in the economy mode for diesel engines. The more weight the engine has to pull, the more fuel it uses.

❑ Always expect road construction when you travel—you won't be disappointed!

❑ If you get a flat tire on the road, first of all move out of traffic lanes. Then decide if you will change it yourself, use an emergency road service, or look up a local service or truck service center. Many people with Type C motorhomes or trailers or fifth wheels can change a flat tire themselves as if it were a car tire. If you decide to change the tire yourself, consult the owner's manual, then see if your vehicle is equipped with the tools you need. If you have an emergency road service plan with an organization such as AAA, Good Sam, or Family Motor Coach Association, you can call the organization for help. Otherwise, search out a local service center. For a heavy RV, you will probably need to find a truck service center.

❏ On a road with three lanes, consider which lane you want to drive in. By driving in the right-hand lane, you have to watch for traffic on only one side. On the other hand, if you drive in the middle lane, trucks and faster traffic can pass you from the rear on either side.

❏ Try to keep your last travel day short. If you arrive home by midafternoon, you'll be able to unload in daylight and do all the necessary tasks when you're not weary from a long day's travel.

❏ If you don't keep your headlights on all the time, be sure to turn them on when it rains. In many states, you're required to do so.

❏ When it's time to fuel the RV, choose a gas station carefully. Using a gas station on the right side of the street is easier than crossing traffic. Before pulling up to the pump, check to see how the station is laid out. Is the roof over the pumps high enough to clear the fifth wheel or motorhome? Is there enough room to maneuver to and from the gas pumps? Are the entrance and exit level enough that the rear hitch on the motorhome won't drag on the ground?

❏ Truck stop stores carry all kinds of merchandise that truckers (or tourists) might need or want—from travel logs to clothes to snacks and souvenirs. And of course the adjoining restaurants usually serve good food because that's especially important to people making their living on the road.

❏ If your new motorhome is getting terrible gas mileage, don't despair. Once the coach is broken in, you can expect better mileage. (One trucker reported that he started to get maximum mileage when his vehicle's odometer read 30,000 miles.)

❏ Keep a calculator handy in a dashboard compartment so you can quickly figure gas mileage. Divide the number of gallons of gas purchased into the number of miles traveled since the last fill-up.

❏ Truck stops stay open all night. You can buy a directory (see the appendix) that lists the locations of truck stops across the country.

Diesel Engines and Refueling

❏ Buy diesel fuel at truck stops and high-volume distributors because it minimizes the chance of water in the diesel fuel. If water gets into the fuel, it will shut down the engine.

—Curtis Greene (CG), Service Manager, Endless Summer RV's, Frederick, MD

❏ One major benefit of an RV with a diesel engine is that all engine noise is in the rear of the motorhome, not in the driver's area. Also, there is normally more storage room in the basement compartments, which is especially useful for full-timers. You can have larger floor plans and more and larger slideouts with greater carrying capacity.

—CG

❏ Here are several other reasons for choosing an RV with a diesel engine instead of a gasoline engine:

1. Diesel engines provide better overall performance as related to power and weight.

2. The engine lasts longer.

3. The inside floor layout is on one level.

4. You get better handling and steering.

5. Most have an air suspension system.

6. The unit has a greater gross combined vehicle weight rating.

7. There's a longer period between most maintenance requirements.

8. Diesel fuel is not as volatile as gasoline (it combusts at a higher temperature).

❑ The diesel fuel-dispensing equipment at a truck stop is faster than that at an automobile service station because the dispensing nozzle and hose are designed for a greater volume for flow.

❑ If you overfill with diesel fuel at a truck stop, instead of wiping off the fuel spilled on the motorhome with a cloth, take the water hose nearby and wash down the area and then wipe it dry. This will prevent dirt in the diesel fuel or on the side of the coach from scratching the paint.

———— ◇ ————

A Farewell in Arms

ALMOST BEFORE WE knew it, our reunion was drawing to a close. And so, on a hot September Saturday afternoon, Jackie Wrigley drove Mary Jo Cornell and me in her car into Petaluma to scout out a restaurant for our farewell dinner that evening.

We stopped at the visitor center for restaurant suggestions. We went into several restaurants to see what they were like, including the River House Restaurant on Weller Street. It was closed during the afternoon, but the owner happened to be outside working on the landscaping. He kindly took us inside and showed us through the five dining rooms of the stately 1888 Queen Anne Victorian mansion. The menu sounded enticing, so we made reservations for eight people for 5:30 that evening.

We arrived at the River House Restaurant in two cars. The maître d' showed us to a private niche on the second floor overlooking the Petaluma River, where we could watch the setting sun and its reflection on the water.

We assembled around a long table covered with a white cloth, crystal wine goblets, tall water glasses, four-piece place settings, and three bud vases of fresh flowers. Photographs of Petaluma scenes hung on the off-white walls. Spouses sat across the table from spouses.

The dinner conversation was animated. Then, after dinner, came that moment when our thoughts turned from our group activities to getting back on the road and the conversation paused. Someone said something about the road conditions. Another talked about the weather forecast. We were delaying the inevitable. We had enjoyed our time together, but it was time to leave the table.

We left the River House Restaurant after eight o'clock, well satisfied with our choice of restaurants. Bill and Mary Jo rode with Jackie and Lyle back to the campground while Paul and I returned there with Lib and John.

Paul and I went about preparing to leave in the morning. He dumped the gray and black water tanks and disconnected the sewer hose and put it away. Not only would the reduced weight from the liquid result in better fuel mileage but draining the holding tanks would prepare us to boondock at our next stop. I brought the travel log up to date by listing what we had spent that day. I went around the interior of the motorhome putting away what was out of place and inserted the map that I would use the next day in the wooden file box beside my navigator's chair. After making sure the path was clear, Paul pushed the switch that brought the slideout inside and locked it for traveling on the road.

I was too tired to write in my computer journal and went to bed instead. I set the alarm on our small clock—we and the Graybeals planned to get an early start in the morning.

At seven o'clock on Sunday morning, Paul unhooked our white water hose from the campground faucet and our heavy black electric cable from the campground electrical outlet and stored them both in their respective outside compartments. I sat in the passenger seat in the dark with the camera hanging from a strap around my neck, ready to say good-bye to our fellow Alaskan caravaners.

Outside, daylight broke. A few people wearing sweaters and sitting on lawn chairs across the road enjoyed the early morning quiet beside a small campfire.

Then I saw Lib walking up the road to Mary Jo and Bill's cedar split-log cabin. I joined her and Mary Jo inside. Bill was taking a shower down at the bathhouse, Mary Jo said. We laughed and talked about the events of the last 10 days.

We hugged good-bye, then Lib and I walked down the slight incline to our motorhomes. By that time, Jackie and Lyle were outside talking with John and Paul. They wished us a good, safe trip and thanked us for our part in the reunion.

Paul and I returned to our motorhome. Although I was sure that Paul wanted to drive, I asked him if he would like me to do so. Without hesitation, he said no but that he was glad to have that option.

I sat again in the navigator's seat. I had the wooden file box next to the seat as usual, but I still had ample leg room. Unlike in our previous coach, there was no center engine hump between the driver's and navigator's seats since the diesel engine (as well as the engine noise) was at the rear of the motorhome. At 7:23, we pulled out of our site, waving good-bye to Jackie and Lyle. I thought of their warm, generous friendship and hoped they would find their way easily and safely to Arizona and then Florida.

We drove past Bill, back from the shower and standing near the cabin. With the sun shining through the morning mist, he smiled, waved to us, and mouthed something like "Safe trip" as we crunched past him on the gravel road.

For the first time during 27 travel days, Paul and I would park our motorhome overnight in a stranger's driveway.

When we planned to attend the Alaskan RV Caravaners reunion in California, we knew the Graybeals wanted to visit their friends Jackie and Paul Cauwels in Merced, California. Paul was a former student of John's in high school in Maryland. The Cauwelses had insisted there was plenty of room in their driveway for both our motorhomes and the tow car. Still, I felt uneasy about imposing on them.

The sun shone brightly just above the horizon as the Graybeals and we reached SR 101 South on the first day of October. Even so, Paul had his headlights on for visibility. We drove with Paul in the lead motorhome and the Graybeals following at a safe distance.

We had refueled the motorhome when we left Marina. Before turning into the service station there, Paul and I both checked to be sure the entrance and exits were level enough so that the rear hitch of the motorhome did not drag and that the canopy was sufficiently high for our rig to pass beneath. At that time, I calculated our miles per gallon. I always keep a calculator within reach of the navigator's seat for this purpose. Paul was pleased with the result of 12.05 miles per gallon of diesel fuel. During our travel to Merced, we would not need to stop for fuel.

At nine o'clock we saw a sign warning "Gusty Wind Area" and drove along gaping at swirling windmills on the ridges of mountains. We drove over Altamont Pass, elevation 1,009 feet.

When we reached Merced, John took the lead since he knew the way to Paul Cauwels's home. After many turns, we arrived at the Cauwelses', a lovely rambling Dutch Colonial–style home with an attached garage set back the length of a football field from the street. The long, concrete-curbed driveway contained stone chips and looked wide enough for even three motorhomes to be parked side by side.

The Graybeals unhooked the tow car, backed their motor-home into the driveway, and stopped just in front of a two-story barn. They parked the tow car beside their motorhome. Then Paul backed our coach in and parked on the opposite side of the driveway just ahead of the double-car garage door, leaving space for a vehicle to pass when the slideout was extended.

Paul Cauwels helped to get each motorhome plugged into electricity from his house. He had heavy duty electric cables as did both the Graybeals and we.

Next, we all piled into Paul and Jackie's Cadillac sport utility vehicle and headed for the Cauwelses' cabin in the mountains near Mariposa. A great tour guide, Paul showed us the Old Stone Jail and the oldest county courthouse in operation in the United States in Mariposa, California. Since both the Cauwelses and the Graybeals were interested in antiques, we stopped at an antique store in Mariposa. I ended up buying five Zane Grey books.

We drove toward the cabin on a mountain road through ever-green forests. Paul and Jackie had been working almost feverishly on building and furnishing a large two-story Dutch Colonial cabin on a lot in the woods on the top of a mountain. I marveled at their handiwork and their use of antiques.

On Monday, Paul and I had no set schedule. John and Lib went golfing with Paul Cauwels and a friend from Australia, while Jackie taught her English as a Second Language class.

Paul worked around our motorhome, doing what he calls "normal maintenance." He cleaned the lenses on the taillights, turn signals, headlights, marker lights on the sides, side-view mirrors, and windshield. He checked the air pressure in all six tires. He also checked all the lights and turn signals to be sure they lit properly. He checked the oil and drained the water from the fuel/water separator.

I wrote to my heart's content in my computer journal. Later that morning, I enjoyed a brisk walk outdoors on a nearby bike path.

About seven, we all gathered in the dining room. Jackie had tossed a huge bowl of salad to go with her specialty—lasagna. To my astonishment, she had sieved the seeds out of the tomatoes in the lasagna so that my husband could eat it. (Paul is not supposed to eat seeds, nuts, or corn because of diverticulosis.) She also served him fresh sliced peaches instead of the boysenberries that she served the rest of us for dessert with cake and vanilla ice cream.

The sun had gone down, but about 8:15, Paul Cauwels took the Graybeals and us a few miles away to see an ostrich farm. When we arrived, Pat Telling, the co-owner of Aussie's Ostriches, came to greet us. She was sorry that her husband, David, was not there, but she offered to show us what she could in the dark with her flashlight.

We walked a few steps to a fenced pen where one-and-a-half-week-old ostrich chicks clustered for warmth under a brooder. Pat transferred one of the chicks into my cupped hands—a reddish-blonde chick with a grayish-white bib, or so it appeared at night. Its long neck and wide-eyed head churned quickly, inquisitively.

Soft down covered its underbelly. On top, longer feathers prickled my fingers.

Pat led us to other pens with older ostriches, who had settled down for the night. When the light from her flashlight and the flash from my camera roused them, they rose easily to their magnificent height and began loping between stalls. Their strides seemed gigantic.

Pat and Dave made sure we got some ostrich burgers to take with us. Ostrich meat has relatively little fat—it is called the "alternative red meat" and tastes somewhat like beef. (See Dave's recipe for ostrich burgers in the appendix.) We were able to fit her generous supply of patties in our freezers, although we didn't have room for much else.

Back at the Cauwelses', we sat in the family room with Jackie, laughing and enjoying one another's conversation. Paul Cauwels served almonds and sodas and sat in what must have been his favorite old rocking chair. It reminded me of the ones that my mother had in her living room.

About 10:15, we hugged and said our good-byes. Jackie and Paul both had obligations early the next morning. They invited us to come back on another trip when they would show us more of the area—Sonora, Yosemite, and other places, including the ostrich farm in the daylight.

On Tuesday morning, Paul unhooked our electric cord from the Cauwelses' heavy duty extension cord in their large double-car garage and lowered the white overhead garage door. John taped to the door a sheet of white paper on which he had printed a large "Thank you!" with the notation "Best campground on trip." He added all four of our names, the time, and date.

It was a sunny, warm morning without a breeze as John and Lib hooked up the tow car to the Southwind. Our caravan slowly ground forward on the wide chipped stone driveway. I felt good about our first experience of staying overnight in a stranger's driveway. The amazing part was how graciously the Cauwelses had incorporated the four of us into their busy schedules and how they had treated Paul and me as if they had known us forever. They had opened not only their driveway and house to us but also their hearts.

12

Navigating

HOW MANY times have you heard or said, "You can't get there from here"? Navigation is key when heading out in an RV. Finding your way can be scary and mysterious; you can and will get lost. And although map reading comes easier to some people than others, road maps and atlases are necessary tools. Here are some tips to help you stay on the beaten path (as long as that's where you want to be).

❑ When you are staying with friends in their driveway, identify a billboard or another landmark to look for to know when to turn onto their street or road. This is especially helpful at night.
—Annie Carroll, Panama City, FL

❑ Learn how to read a road map. The legend on the map will show you what all the different symbols mean. It may indicate scenic routes and exit numbers too. You should also find symbols for rest areas and picnic areas and even campgrounds.

❑ Before hitting the road in the morning, get out the maps and tour books you'll want during that day, as well as the campground directory. You'll be glad to have them handy when a question comes up.

❏ Keep your map folded open to the relevant section.

❏ Use a yellow felt tip pen to highlight the next day's route on your map. This helps the navigator follow the route and give information to the driver as requested.

❏ Write down the day's route numbers for the other drivers in your caravan if you are the one who figured out the itinerary. Having information written down makes navigation easier. Discuss and review your notes with the other drivers also.

❏ Lost? Don't panic. Look at the map and ask for directions at the nearest gas station.

❏ In addition to carrying campground and truck stop directories with you, stop at city and state visitor centers, talk to campground hosts, and pick up maps of the area and brochures on what to see and do.

❏ Get a map of each state you will drive through either from your automobile association before you leave home or at the welcome center for that state (where they are free). A state map is usually larger than the page in an atlas and contains more information such as smaller towns. Atlases do come in handy when route planning involves several states at once, and because of their size, they are easy to handle.

❏ Be sure your state maps show rest areas and exit numbers. This helps you to plan stops as you travel. Some highway signs will tell you the distance to the next rest area.

❏ Navigators should be able to tell the driver what the exit numbers are so the driver will know when to leave the interstate highway. Also, by knowing the last exit number before leaving some states, you can determine how many more miles you will travel in that state on that highway. For example, in Mississippi, the last exit number for I-10 as shown on the map is Exit 75. As we traveled east on I-10 toward that exit, we passed a sign for Exit 61. We subtracted 61 from 75 and learned that we had 14 more miles in Mississippi.

Sedona

A COUSIN WHO traveled in a motorhome had raved to me about some spectacular red rocks at Sedona, Arizona. I pictured a few brownish-red rocks jutting out near a mountain road. Then other travelers to the area exclaimed about their beauty and tried to describe their magnificence. I sensed something unique and awesome about those red rocks that I wanted to see. And so Paul and I planned to visit Sedona when we took a southern route back home through Arizona.

When we left Merced on that Tuesday morning, we took Route 99 south toward Bakersfield.

After lunch in our motorhomes in a rest area between Tulare and Tipton, the four of us conferred in the Graybeals' coach. We agreed to stop in Bakersfield for fuel, the Graybeals for gasoline and we for diesel. Since some gasoline stations do not offer diesel fuel, Paul looked in our truck stop directory and found five truck stops in the Bakersfield area. If we got separated from one another, we would meet south of Bakersfield at a rest area near Boron. We also decided to stop that night at a campground in Adelanto, California. So with our route planned for that day, we headed back on the road.

Paul and I work as a team when navigating. When I first began traveling in the motorhome, I didn't know how to read a road map. Riding in an automobile, I usually didn't pay much attention to directions. With motorhome travel, Paul began to ask for information from the map. He also asked me to help him look at road signs for route numbers or city names.

With practice, I learned to use the road map to find exit numbers, rest areas, picnic areas, and large towns that lay ahead. Maps have more information than I realized. They give distances between points, show scenic routes, and graphically indicate whether a road is a dual highway or a dirt road.

It turned out that both the Graybeals and we filled our motorhome fuel tanks at the Flying J Truck Stop at Merced Avenue in Bakersfield. In Bakersfield we left Route 99 and took Route 58. Shortly, I saw the peaks of the Sierra Nevada on the left, in a misty vagueness. We began to leave the level valley with irrigated farm crops and orchards and head into the mountains. Still shrouded, the mountains became clearer as we got nearer.

We headed toward Tehachapi Summit at 4,064 feet in the southern Sierra Nevada. John said that his engine was running the hottest it had since he left home.

Route 58 took us down into a canyon between the hills of the Sierra Nevada. The town of Tehachapi lay off to our right in a wide valley.

We descended into the Mojave Desert and passed the town of Mojave. To our right in the distance was Edwards Air Force Base, where the space shuttles land when Florida has bad weather. Paul asked me for detailed directions from the campground directory to the campground in Adelanto. We found SR 395 and made our way to Adelanto RV Park & Resort. We were in high desert country. The wind blew the leaves vigorously on the deciduous and evergreen trees in the park.

That campground deserved its high rating in the directory. Interior roads were wide and asphalted and sites had concrete patios and gravel instead of grass. The store and laundry were topnotch. The campground was surrounded by the desert, which lay just beyond a perimeter fence with a pet gate.

The next morning, Wednesday, Day 30 of our trip, we continued to drive through the high desert terrain. Although we had arrived at Adelanto on SR 395, we departed it on Route 18 toward Victorville.

Route 18 was a beautiful drive in the sense of spectacular rocky foothills and unexpected blooming flowers in landscaped lawns of homes in the midst of the desert environment. Traffic was moderate with cars and a few trucks on the two-lane paved road. Occasional Joshua trees stood guard over the other desert clumps of dried brush.

At Lucerne Valley, we left Route 18 and continued east instead on Route 247 just outside the town. I didn't mind driving through the seemingly isolated desert because I knew that we could boondock if necessary. I enjoyed the feel of being in the desert with its isolation and unseen fauna.

We descended an eight-degree grade into Yucca Valley, which gave us a spectacular view of a wide, desert valley. Soon after reaching the city of Yucca Valley, we turned onto Route 62.

As we continued on Route 62 on a rolling valley road, we again saw stands of swirling windmills on the right. All shapes, sizes, and heights livened the desert hills and fields. A yellow sign warned "Gusty Wind Area" ahead. I felt our rig shifting in the wind. Paul worked at keeping the coach centered in his lane.

At the end of Route 62 we turned right onto the ramp for I-10 East. We passed Palm Springs, which was hidden behind rows of trees at the side of the interstate.

I checked the campground directory for possible sites in Quartzsite, Arizona. We chose the Holiday Palms, which had a high rating. It was also a Good Sam Park and gave a 10 percent discount to members, which we were.

At 1:51 that afternoon, we crossed the Colorado River. Halfway across the bridge we saw a sign: "Arizona State Line." We had also gone from Pacific to Mountain Time.

By 2:15 we arrived at Holiday Palms RV Park, Quartzsite, Arizona. Quartzsite is an important stay en route to Phoenix where people boondock and visit a huge flea market and rock and mineral shows. The population swells from 2,100 to one million people in January and February when these events are held. However, the town appeared almost deserted as we drove into its western end in October.

It was the slow season, of course, for the park. The office was open only until noon daily, but the manager lived next door and made himself available whenever needed.

I did two loads of laundry. The laundry room was not air conditioned and must have been 95 degrees. At times, a breeze came through the window. While the clothes washed, I went outside to the pay phone and made my daily calls for messages.

Meantime, Paul helped John take apart a connector to his rear brake and turn signal lights to figure out why the lights sometimes failed. They found a defect in the wiring between the motorhome and the tow vehicle and repaired it.

Later, John drove the four of us to Ted's Truck Center just up the street. It contains an enormous restaurant with the authentic atmosphere of a truck stop. The menu plainly stated that truckers get first priority in service. A special area was set aside for drivers. The parking area was busy with big tractor-trailers coming and going.

The next morning, shortly before eight o'clock, we left Holiday Palms and drove toward the east end of Quartzsite, which we had not yet seen. We passed empty campsites at campgrounds, ones that would be filled in January and February. Along I-10

East, we drove through a Bureau of Land Management area where winter boondockers would reside in the huge, gravel- and rock-strewn desert on both sides of the road.

The road to Phoenix stretched flat and smooth across the desert. We stopped at the Burnt Well Rest Area, where we found that nearly everything a traveler might need had been thoughtfully provided. In fact, we gave high ratings to all the rest areas we visited in Arizona.

We had driven many miles through desert and yet the scenery continued to fascinate me. The desert landscape, contrary to what one might think, varied with each mile.

At Exit 129 we left the interstate. I read to Paul the directions to the campground from the directory to give him an overview of what to expect. When he asked, I repeated the directions as we drove along.

Since John couldn't see the traffic lights ahead because the height of our rig blocked his view, he asked Paul to let him know whether they were red or green so that he would know when to slow down or stop. Paul was glad to do that.

By 11 o'clock that Thursday morning, we registered in the office at Sunflower Resort in Surprise, Arizona, on the northwestern outskirts of Phoenix. A genial older gentleman led us by golf cart to a site beside the Graybeals. After hooking up our motorhomes to electricity and water, we all went to the Crossroads Shopping Center in Surprise, where we ate lunch and Lib had a manicure, Paul a haircut, and I a shampoo and blow-dry.

The next morning about 7:30, Paul drove me in the Graybeals' car to see the red rocks that everybody raved about. Our friends had also suggested that we visit Montezuma Castle on the way. A perfect day for sightseeing, it was clear and 70 degrees with no breeze. John was up and saw us off, giving us some last-minute sightseeing information.

The road climbed to 4,000 feet. At Exit 289, we left I-17 and followed the signs to Montezuma Castle. A parking lot and visitor center welcomed us. Admission to the trail below the castle ruins was $2.00 per person (children under 17 free). Two busloads of school children were visiting along with us and other tourists. A self-guiding trail took us below the castle and past a scale-model of the interior. Sinagua Indian farmers began building the five-storied structure in a cliff recess 100 feet above the valley in the 12th century. It contained 20 rooms. As I looked up at the rather well-preserved ruins set on the edge of a precipice, I marveled at the bravery and ingenuity of the builders.

The castle got the name "Montezuma" from pioneers who thought Aztecs had built it. Anxious to see the red rocks of Sedona, we did not linger.

At 6,000 feet we entered Coconino County. Continuing uphill, we drove through evergreen forests. The highway leveled off and we began passing ranches with red- and white-faced cattle grazing or lying down in meadows and forests. It was a beautiful drive with pines on both sides, scattered white and gray clouds in the blue sky, and red soil on the banks beside the highway.

A sign said "Flagstaff City Limits." At Flagstaff, we were only about 84 miles from the south rim of the Grand Canyon. Soon, from I-17, we took Exit 337 and followed signs to Route 89A South, or Oak Creek Canyon Drive. Sedona lay 23 miles ahead. I sat up straighter in the passenger seat and looked in all directions for red rocks.

We descended into Oak Creek Canyon on a winding road. Switchbacks wound down to a canyon floor that still had an elevation of 6,000 feet. I gasped at unusual rock formations on the right—but not yet red ones.

We passed a small brown building labeled "Sedona Fire Department." And then we began to see red rocks on our right. A few minutes later, more red rocks appeared on the left.

We continued on the winding Oak Creek Canyon Drive. Closer to Sedona, it led us among and beside towering vermilion cliffs, rouge buttes, and other huge rock formations.

Mouths gaping, we entered the mile-long main street of Sedona. On our left, I caught glimpses of more red rocks rising beyond the buildings of the town.

We melded into busy traffic. In sunshine, the walks on both sides of the street were peppered with people who walked in and out of the various stores and restaurants.

At the south end of Sedona, I obtained an official guide and other tourist information from the Oak Creek Chamber of Commerce. From the attendant, I learned that the red rocks were *not* all clustered in one place, nor can they all be seen from one location. Rather, tourists can fan out from Sedona on their own tour or can take guided tours of all kinds—Jeep, horseback, hiking, and van tours. You can fly over the area in an airplane, a helicopter, or even in a hot air balloon. The town itself offers a trolley. You can spend several days touring the area.

After lunch in Sedona, knowing our time was limited, we headed to see more of the rocks instead of the shops and galleries in town. A woman at the tourist center had recommended that we see the rocks from the Chapel of the Holy Cross, which was off of Route 179 on Chapel Road.

While Paul stayed in the car in the parking area, I walked up the rather steep road, then on a wide, winding ramp to the top of a hill, where the Chapel of the Holy Cross stood, commanding a viewpoint. I noticed that cars could drive to the top if necessary. The chapel was flanked by spectacular red rocks.

It was almost three o'clock when I entered the small, modern chapel. Through what seemed like a five-story-high window with vertical panels of clear glass, I looked onto tops of nearby red-rock mountains and distant tree-covered hills. A blue sky served as backdrop for fragments of white clouds, barely moving.

I sat and breathed it all in. The choir chanted and a bell rang. I closed my eyes to pray.

Outside the chapel, the red rocks included formations called the Two Nuns and Bell Rock. Their color and surface made me think of the soft, fine patina of cosmetic rouge. The size of those huge mounds of colorful stone was breathtaking. Reluctantly, I left that temple area, walked back down the ramp and road, and rejoined Paul.

"I think seeing these rocks was well worth the trip," I said. I could never have imagined how awe-inspiring they are. Paul agreed.

13

Coping in the Kitchen: Food, Water, and Entertaining

W HEN IT comes to meals on the road, RVers abide by one rule: the simpler, the better. Friends and family know to expect casual fare, whether for a meal or an impromptu snack. Here are some tips to help you further simplify kitchen chores.

❏ Be sure to stock plenty of s'mores-making supplies. They are really expensive in the camping supply stores. (S'mores are sandwiches made of graham crackers, chocolate bars, and marshmallows toasted over a campfire.)
   —Lorraine Jones, Westminster, MD

❏ Keep all sandwich-making items in a plastic container in the refrigerator to cut down on opening and closing the door. Group other supplies in the same manner. Take along canned carbonated beverages instead of bottled. Pressure builds up with vehicle motion and tops can blow off bottles.
   —Herb and Mary-Lou Pletcher, Taneytown, MD

❏ To save work and still feed everyone well, cook a large beef roast a day or two before you leave. Chop the leftover meat into pieces and take it with you. Add gravy and a can of mixed vegetables and you have instant stew.

Add a salad and fruit and your meal is done. If you have more beef than needed for stew, slice it for sandwiches. You could also cook a chicken and debone it. You then have meat for chicken sandwiches and broth for soup. Refrigerator space is usually limited in an RV, so package perishables in as small a container as you can. Doing advance preparation makes for carefree time for the cook. Chili or vegetable soup are also good to prepare in advance.

—Emagene Yingling, Edinburg, TX

❏ To save space that a large grill would take up, carry along a cast-iron skillet and a backpacker's grill (which has four hinged legs that are shoved into the ground so you can control the height). Line the skillet with aluminum foil, spread briquettes in it and soak them with starter fluid, then light them. When the coals are hot, put the backpacker's grill over the skillet and grill anything you wish. When finished, pour water over the coals to extinguish them. When they're cold, fold the aluminum foil over the top and discard the package—easy cleanup.

—Larry and Patricia Olson, Webb, IA

❏ Meat keeps better if it's frozen in the house before leaving home.

—Charlene Schweikhart, Indianapolis, IN

❏ When transporting fruit and vegetables in an RV, package them so that they do not move around. Rolling and bumping can cause bruising, which may hasten deterioration.

—Donna Scott, Food Safety Specialist, Cornell University, Ithaca, NY

❏ Unless you have a filtering system in your RV, you'll want to carry gallon (or larger) jugs of drinking water with you. Refill the jugs at rest area spigots, campground faucets where the water is potable, and at the homes of people you visit along the way.

❑ When you shop for groceries during the trip, pick out the frozen items last. They'll be that much colder when you get them back to the RV.

❑ Your RV's refrigerator is already small. Don't let it fill up with old leftovers no one will ever eat or soda bottles with two sips left in them. Sort through the contents regularly.

❑ Entertaining in an RV comes without the stress and anxiety that one suffers at home, where the house must be perfect, clothes right for the occasion, and food extra-ordinary. On the road, people expect everything to be casual—living quarters, traveling clothes, and meals. Informality and understanding come with the territory.

❑ Whether entertaining at home or on the road, the principle is the same: do as much as possible ahead of time so you can enjoy the company of your guests when they arrive.

❑ Although the actual space in an RV kitchen is quite small, you'll manage quite well if you make sure the counter is cleared off and the sink is free of dirty dishes before you begin to cook.

<>

Entertaining In

OUR NEW MOTORHOME is perfect for entertaining. A 37-foot Holiday Rambler Endeavor, its living room area enlarges 20 inches when we extend the slideout. Not only does the added space give elbow room to Paul and me when parked at night, but it allows all our guests to gather in a centralized area.

Just as at home, I like to serve food that delights our guests. While no one expects a pastry chef's signature dessert on the road, I want to serve something that guests enjoy. Uncertainty always flares up inside me when I plan food for visitors, whether at home or in the motorhome. I agree with those who say that the hardest part about hosting is deciding what food to serve. Once decided, however, I love to entertain people in our motorhome. When they simply drop by, I just serve whatever I have on hand.

Late on a sunny Saturday morning, on October 7, Day 33, the Graybeals and we pulled out of our sites at the Sunflower Resort, Surprise, Arizona.

Soon we reached I-10 East and headed toward New Mexico. We left behind the city milieu of the Phoenix area and drove through desert with sandy soil and sagebrush. Mountains lay in the distance all around. Some of the level fields along the road were plowed, and some irrigated ones contained cotton ready to pick.

We passed Willcox. The highway was smooth, but the cross-wind gusted against the rig with such force that Paul had to be constantly alert to his driving.

At 4:15 that afternoon, New Mexico, the "Land of Enchantment," welcomed us. The arid terrain and wind continued. We passed a small Type C motorhome parked beside I-10 as the owner strove to wind up an awning that had come unfurled in the strong wind.

By five o'clock, Paul was registering at the Lordsburg KOA Kampground. Tired from the struggle of driving in the wind that day, Paul said that he wanted to eat in the motorhome, which was fine with the Graybeals. I fixed two hearty frozen entrées in the microwave.

After dinner, John came over with handwritten information on travel for the next two days. Paul and I reviewed it—we really appreciated having directions written down.

By 7:30 on Sunday morning, we were cruising on I-10, our destination that day being Fort Stockton, Texas. It would be a full day of driving.

We crossed the Continental Divide, elevation 4,585 feet, about eight o'clock. The dual highway was smooth. We saw cloudy skies and a fine rain on the windshield. The wipers moved back and forth in their regular rhythm. After a couple of hours more, we were in Texas.

That afternoon, it rained off and on. We passed ranches and dry draws, buttes and mesas, and drove miles and miles on a straight road.

Shortly after five o'clock, we turned into Fort Stockton KOA Kampground. The rain continued as we waited in line to register.

Paul and John drove 410 miles that Sunday, Day 34. Needless to say, we ate in and relaxed that evening.

The next day, October 9th, marked Paul's and my 52nd wedding anniversary.

As we headed toward San Antonio, Paul and I rode along, content with the road, the countryside, and our relationship. It's special to have a husband who has a good spirit of generosity, forgiveness, and humor and who looks on the positive side of life. I feel blessed to be married to Paul. He has idiosyncracies that I've accommodated to, but I have more. We accept one another "as is" and make the most of what we have that we like.

We parked that afternoon in cold, damp weather at Alamo Fiesta RV Resort (Boerne, Texas), side by side with the Graybeals. That arrangement had worked quite well during the trip.

John called Fred Martin and arranged for us to meet him at the resort's office. Fred and his wife, Judy, had been students in John's twelfth-grade Problems of Democracy class at North Carroll High School in Hampstead, Maryland. Retired now, they live in Fair Oaks.

Fred and Judy drove all of us in their white Cadillac to the Old San Francisco Steak House. We walked under a canopy into another era—the gay 1890s.

The huge, low-lit room was filled with diners and the sounds of laughter and talking. We arrived just as the "Girl in the Red Velvet Swing" climbed into a swing suspended from the 30-foot ceiling.

She wore a short red dress trimmed with a white feather boa around her shoulders, black net stockings, and red pumps with ankle straps. As she swung back and forth, she looked at the audience and smiled broadly. Her goal was to swing high enough to ring a bell hanging from the ceiling on each side of the stage. We watched expectantly as she went higher and higher. When she rang the bell with her foot, everyone applauded. She did this several times and then gradually came to a standstill, hopped off the swing, and bowed to the audience, which applauded enthusiastically. She proceeded to give several children a few swings on the swing.

Back at our table, someone made a toast to Paul and me. During the meal, Paul walked to the stage and asked the pianist to play the "Anniversary Waltz." When we finished the entrée, several servers came to the table with a cake and sang "Happy Anniversary" to us. What a happy, memorable occasion our friends gave to us!

The following evening, Judy and Fred came by about 5:45 in their SUV. We all went to dinner at My Back Porch in Boerne, less than a mile from our campground. This time, Paul and I rode with the Martins, and the Graybeals rode in their car. (Neither of our vehicles held six people comfortably.)

Paul and I invited everyone back to our motorhome for dessert. When Judy and Fred entered our motorhome, we gave them a tour of the place. I had already laid out on the dining table dessert forks and spoons, dessert plates, mugs, napkins, and a knife to cut the two Pepperidge Farm cakes that Paul and I bought earlier that day at the H-E-B store in Boerne.

John and Lib arrived with a pot of coffee and extra forks and spoons. Our guests made themselves comfortable in the living room area of the motorhome while Paul and I served the cake and coffee.

Fred told us about his and Judy's experience with the Kairos prison ministry. Twice a year they spend a weekend visiting with prisoners. The four of us sat enthralled as we listened to Fred and Judy talk about the program and their part in it. All too soon, they had to leave. The Martins wished us a safe journey, then drove away into the night.

The Graybeals went home next door with their coffeepot, silverware, and some cake. Paul and I did the dishes. It had been a good day.

14

Staying in Touch: Telephones and Mail

WHEN YOU dream of RVing, you think of getting away from the demands of the telephone and mail. Once on the road, however, you find yourself making telephone calls and looking for post offices to mail cards and letters. Keeping in contact with friends and family is easier when you follow the advice of experienced travelers.

❑ Before you go on a trip, print out small adhesive labels addressed to the people you want to send postcards to. As you find cards you like, simply affix a stamp and preprinted label, then write a personal note. When the labels are all gone, you'll know you've written to everyone that you promised to.

—Debra Draper, Yorba Linda, CA

❑ When making several telephone calls at a pay phone using a telephone calling card, you can save the cost and bother of re-entering your number each time if, instead of hanging up, you press the pound (#) sign for two seconds after the first call. A message will ask you to enter the number you wish to call. Simply enter the next number on your list.

❑ As you cruise through small towns at a slower speed, look for post offices. They are easier to spot there than in cities—just look for the U.S. flag.

❑ When you hope to visit friends or relatives en route and plan to call them a day ahead, *before* calling, figure out approximately when you will arrive at their residence so they can arrange their schedule accordingly.

❑ You do not need a credit card to call long distance if the area code is 800, 866, 877, or 888. These numbers are all toll free. (The list of toll-free area codes is continually growing as the demand increases.)

❑ Keep in touch with your family in several ways:

  1. Tell your family members to give messages to the person who is handling your mail. When you call that mail person every few days to ask about mail and business matters, you'll get messages from your family members too.

  2. If you have an answering machine or message service, family members can leave messages there and you can call to retrieve them.

  3. In case of emergency, those to whom you give your cell telephone number can dial that number to reach you.

  4. Use a mail or message service offered by an organization such as the Family Motor Coach Association.

❑ While I usually find a pay phone to make telephone calls because it is more economical for us, it can be convenient and extremely useful to carry a cellular telephone with you. They are especially appreciated when the weather is cold or rainy or when the pay phone is a long distance from where you are parked.

❑ On long trips you can avoid letting your credit card balance build up by calling your credit card company to get your current balance. Ask what you need to send along with your check—usually your account number, name, and address. Keep copies of all receipts, of course.

❑ Before leaving home, shop for greeting cards you'll need on the trip—birthday, Valentine's Day, even get well and sympathy cards just in case. At home, you know where to find just the right cards for the special people in your life.

❑ When using a pay phone to call ahead for reservations, don't forget to take along change or a calling card as well as a credit card in case you need to make a deposit to hold the reservation.

❑ At some truck stops you can find restaurant tables with a telephone—a great convenience compared to a regular pay phone.

❑ If you plan to mail several packages along the way, buy a few priority stamps so that you can drop the packages in a mailbox and avoid a long wait at the post office.

Revisiting Louisiana

A MINUTE BEFORE eight o'clock on a cloudy, 55-degree morning, Paul and I left the Alamo Fiesta RV Resort in Boerne, Texas. It was Day 37 on our journey. The Graybeals and we were headed for Louisiana where, in Cajun country, we hoped to visit Yvonne and Wil Foreman, fellow caravaners to Alaska who had not attended the reunion in California. In eastern Louisiana, we hoped to visit Vera and Earl Mitchell. Earl is a former pastor of the Westminster Church of the Brethren and performed the marriage ceremony for Paul and me 52 years earlier.

That day we drove through the Hill country and East Texas with its picturesque Longhorn and other cattle ranches, green vegetation in large fields, and live oaks and other shade trees. Wildflowers with tiny yellow blossoms brightened the roadsides.

East of Houston, Paul said, "Remind me to clean the side-view mirrors when we get to the next rest stop."

I reached for a jacket and book nearby and piled them on the floor where one of us would have to step over them to go to the rear of the coach. I was careful not to block the exit out of the rig. That pile would remind us to clean the mirror. The reminder worked, and Paul happily cleaned the mirrors at the next place we parked.

By four o'clock, we had reached Orange, Texas, on the border with Louisiana, and Paul and John registered for one night at the Oak Leaf Park Campground. Lib and I waited in our rigs. Two gray speckled quails jerked their heads as they walked across the road in front of our coaches.

After hooking up to utilities, the Graybeals, Paul, and I sat outside at the weathered-gray, wooden picnic table between our coaches and planned our activities for the next few days. We concluded that John would call their friends in Panama City, Florida, and I would call the Foremans; the Mitchells in Slidell, Louisiana; and our niece in Panama City, Florida, to see when it would be convenient to visit.

Before we called, however, we looked at John's atlas and figured out the distances and times that we might visit folks. I had learned from experience that it would save calling again if we could be rather specific about the time of our arrival on the initial call.

It turned out that all were at home and would be happy to have us visit. So for the next day, Thursday, we planned to join the Foremans for lunch at a restaurant in Crowley and then drive to Slidell for a visit with the Mitchells in the evening.

The next morning, about 7:30, I stepped down out of our motorhome and walked in the direction that I thought was the office. With postcards in hand to mail and camera dangling from my neck, I passed John outside his coach dumping the gray and black water tanks.

"Good morning, John!" I said cheerfully. He smiled and said the same to me. I walked down one long shaded avenue, turned right and walked down another, and turned right again, with each turn expecting to see the office ahead. I met a man striding toward me and asked him where the office was.

"Well, you go around this curve and then it's a straight line, then you go down a long street to the office," he said.

I thanked him and I went around a couple more curves. I was about to give up and go back, but eventually I came to the long street. I looked across it to my right. There was *our* motorhome! I had come around a giant loop and was right back where I started.

After mailing my cards, I talked to the woman in the office and asked her if she had owned the campground 10 years earlier. When she said yes, I told her Paul and I had stayed there on our first major trip in our first motorhome.

Shortly after leaving Orange, Texas, we crossed the border. "Welcome to Louisiana, Bievenue en Louisiane," a sign read. We had entered the Cajun area of Louisiana.

About nine o'clock, I called Yvonne Foreman on the cell phone to let her know that we had passed Lake Charles and would be arriving an hour early, about 10 o'clock instead of eleven.

When our small caravan exited I-10 and went down a ramp into Crowley, we could not find the right streets. Once again, I called Yvonne from the passenger seat in the motorhome. She stayed on the phone with us and directed us through Crowley. Then I looked ahead and saw her tall figure standing on the tree-shaded sidewalk in front of her home with the phone at her ear. She saw us coming down the street and waved.

Yvonne directed us to go around the corner to park. And there, Wil, with slouch hat protecting his bald head from the sun, pointed to where we were to park along the side street. His warm smile was framed by a gray beard.

As we sat on the screened porch at the side of the house, Yvonne told us of her recent telephone conversation with Effie Swagerty. Clem was home from the hospital and getting stronger. We were so glad to learn that.

Then she gave us several suggestions on what to see and do in Louisiana. For that morning, she suggested that she show us the farm she inherited from her father.

About 10 miles out into the country, we turned left onto a road that led to what she called "Le Camp." She has about 200 acres of farmland there that belonged to her family.

A large cabin stood in a picturesque setting beside the Bayou Queue de Tortue. We stood under live oak trees with hanging moss. It was quiet and seemed far away from the world.

We explored the cabin, which was constructed in three stages: The taller part, built first, contained the living room and had been a shed. Then a sloped-roof kitchen was attached to that and attached to the kitchen was a lower-roofed bathroom. Yvonne said that the man who helped her father farm had to take care of the pumps day and night in order to keep the rice fields watered. So the cabin started out as a place for him to stay.

On the way back, we stopped on the gravel road for a short visit with "Du" Guillot, who was leasing the land from Yvonne and was preparing it for a rice crop. He climbed down from his yellow Caterpillar tractor with its scoop plow on the front. Dressed in blue denim overalls and a baseball cap, he smiled as he greeted us. A true Acadian, he speaks French most of the time. A very friendly, sociable, and outgoing man, he invited us to see his farm and said he would make jambalaya for us. We hoped to someday accept his engaging invitation.

From the farm we drove back to Crowley and L'Acadie restaurant. The restaurant had been open only about three months. Our server told me that the owners had traveled to Nova Scotia searching for some of the heritage of their ancestors and brought back recipes for the restaurant, which uses all original Nova Scotian recipes. They also bring in from Nova Scotia fresh seafood, including lobsters, caught by Acadian fishermen from towns such as Comeauville, Saunierville, and Church Point. The food, service, and atmosphere were excellent, and everyone there was very friendly.

Back at the Foremans', we said our good-byes and thanked our hosts.

We found our way from Crowley to I-10. With Paul in the lead, our two motorhomes moved along the interstate, which in some places was supported on concrete pilings as it crossed marshy areas.

Since we did not want to go into New Orleans, we left I-10 at Exit 159 and took I-12. We passed Mandeville and Fontainebleau State Park on the north shore of Lake Pontchartrain, where Paul and I stayed 10 years ago as we searched for a warm place to winter.

On this trip we were staying at the Pine Crest RV Park in Slidell, Louisiana. We registered, drove to our side-by-side sites in the tree-shaded campground, hooked up to utilities, and ate dinner in our motorhomes. Afterward, the four of us left the campground in the tow car. At the last minute, I grabbed the cell phone to take along.

We started toward the Mitchells' in Slidell. I had written down the directions after talking by telephone with both Earl and Vera. Yet we couldn't find a street that was in my notes.

John pulled into a gas station and Paul went inside to ask directions. The two women in the office were new in that part of Slidell and didn't know how to direct him. Fortunately, we had the cell phone and the Mitchells' number with us. As John drove along, Paul relayed directions to him as Earl gave them. To be sure that we would not get lost again, Paul asked Earl to stay on the line. When we pulled up in front of the Mitchells' garage, Paul was still talking on the phone with Earl.

"Well, I'm going to say good-bye now so I can come in and see you!" Paul chuckled.

Laughing, the Graybeals and we walked to the front door, where Earl and Vera stood ready to welcome us. We had visited them two years earlier on our 50th wedding anniversary when we attended another reunion of the Alaskan caravaners hosted by the Foremans.

We introduced Lib and John, then Vera and Earl invited us into their family room. Tall and hale looking, Earl had celebrated his 90th birthday. Vera was 88. With a quick wit, she can laugh at herself and quickly perceives what is funny about a situation. Earl is more serious but also has a positive outlook. So the six of us laughed a lot.

We related our adventures on the road. Paul told them about his Beard genealogy project and how he had contacted "lost" cousins in Chile, South America. They asked about mutual friends and church news and brought us up to date on themselves and their families.

Before we left, Earl said a prayer and Vera gave each couple a generous section of home-baked cake, two yellow plastic net scrubbers, and a Christmas tree ornament, all of which she had made herself.

As John drove us back to the campground, we talked about our time with the Foremans and the Mitchells. Both our visits in Louisiana had touched us immeasurably. Such experiences somehow seem more possible (and affordable) when traveling by recreational vehicle.

15

RV Safety

IT'S A funny thing about safety—we think about it more on the return trip than we do starting out. By the time we reach home, we can recall close calls and lessons learned and instances where taking precautions paid off. Here are some useful ideas to help make your next RV trip a safe one.

❏ Always station someone behind you when backing up so you don't run over or into anything.

—Paul LeClair, Bates Motor Home Rentals of Rapid City,
  Black Hawk, SD

❏ Make sure everyone in the tow vehicle or motorhome, especially children, uses seat belts as you travel on the road so that no one gets hurt when the driver goes around corners or makes a sudden stop.

—Bonnie Talbert, New Windsor, MD

❏ Try to travel in pairs or groups. There really is safety in numbers. If you have to (or prefer to) travel alone, give your itinerary to a friend or relative and check in with that person every couple of days or so. This is especially important if you have any health problems, such as high blood pressure or diabetes. If you break down in an isolated area and you don't check in when expected, your contact can tell authorities where to look for you.

❑ If you must walk inside a motorhome when it is in motion on the highway, hold onto pieces of solid furniture or walls and try to look forward as much as possible to see what curves, hills, or traffic is ahead. A sudden stop can throw you down when you are unaware it's coming. (That happened to me three times before I learned this lesson.) This is especially important for diesel pusher users with air brakes that grab quickly and for motorhomes that do not have tag axles.

❑ Read all operation manuals, especially the safety information in them. Pay attention to the warning symbols ⚠ (a triangle with an exclamation point inside), and follow the instructions.

❑ Wash the windshield every day so that you have a clean windshield for clear vision when driving.

❑ Make sure you know where the RV's main LP gas shutoff valve is located. (Ours is on the outside of the motorhome. I open a small square door and inside that opening is the intake nozzle for the gas. Above that is a small knob that when rotated counterclockwise turns off the gas. A red light glows in an adjacent indicator when the gas is turned on.)

❑ While traveling in cold weather, consider using the heat pump rather than the furnace. The furnace uses propane gas and the wind can blow out the flame, causing noxious fumes. The heat pump, on the other hand, uses electricity, which is furnished by the auxiliary generator when on the road or by the campground's electrical outlet when in camp.

❑ Make sure your RV is equipped with an LP gas detector. Check it regularly (per the manufacturer's instructions) to make sure it's in working order.

❑ Don't let time pressure cause you to take risks in passing other traffic or driving over the posted speed limit. If a campground or friends are expecting you, phone ahead to let them know your time dilemma. Know that it's better to get there late in one piece than not at all.

❑ Drive with the headlights on all the time in order to be highly visible to other traffic and thereby lessen the chances of someone running into your vehicle.

❑ Always lock your RV's door when leaving for the day. Don't assume a traveling companion will do it for you.

❑ When you park your rig, watch out for remnants of old tires. They sometimes contain wire that will damage your tires if you run over them.

❑ When you're traveling in a caravan with another RV, write down the route numbers for the day's travel for each driver. It's easy to forget whether U.S. 84 or U.S. 82 was the right road. Be sure to keep your travel partner's cell phone number handy too, in case you lose contact by CB.

❑ Tune in to local radio occasionally as you travel. If there's a storm warning or other potential emergency, you'll want to know about it. Keep your ears open at gasoline stations and truck stops and you'll hear news about flooded areas and other road hazards.

❑ Be prepared to work with the weather, whatever it turns out to be.

—————— ◇ ——————

Safely Home

SO FAR DURING 38 days of travel from Maryland to California to Slidell, Louisiana, we had kept in touch with one another on the road by Citizens Band radio. Only once did we lose contact, in Arizona, when we stopped for fuel and the Graybeals agreed to go on ahead to the next rest area and wait for us there. The rest area turned out to be quite far beyond where our maps showed it. We briefly feared that we wouldn't find one another until we reached home. On the last part of the journey, I hoped we would not have such anxious moments again.

Our route from Pine Crest RV Park in Slidell took us on I-10, the major interstate highway running west to east through Louisiana, Mississippi, and Alabama into the panhandle of Florida. We would spend the weekend boondocking in Panama City on Saint Andrew Bay in the driveway of Anne and Richard Carroll, friends of the Graybeals.

Originally, Richard had arranged for us to park in his neighbor's driveway, but it turned out that his Newmar Kountry Star 35-foot Class A motorhome could share the wide, concrete driveway with both the Graybeals' Southwind and our Holiday Rambler Endeavor. Richard backed his car out of the garage before directing us into the driveway. Our motorhome was located on the left side of the driveway facing the house and thus we were able to extend the slideout.

Annie is noted as a good cook. For breakfast Saturday morning, she prepared for us a delicious casserole of grits, sausage, mushrooms, eggs, and cheese. We couldn't tell there were any grits in it. She said she'd fooled a number of people who thought they did not like grits.

The next day, Sunday, was a delightful day by the bay—the sun shone, birds sang, and the water was peaceful. We gave the Carrolls a tour of our motorhome and they showed us theirs, which is absolutely beautiful. We enjoyed lingering in the back-yard looking at the water, seeing pelicans, and watching a por-poise surface and dive. Annie made tortilla soup for lunch—a delicious gourmet mixture of ground beef and beans with onion and other seasoning, grated yellow cheese, and a dollop of sour cream.

Annie seems to accomplish tasks effortlessly and with great fun. A loyal Redskins fan, Annie wore a Redskins sweatshirt and cap as she watched the Redskins and Ravens that afternoon. Every time the Redskins scored, she rang a bell. As she enjoyed the game, sweet potatoes baked in a slow oven for three hours. She had previously baked a ham that Richard carved for dinner after the game. She added fancy bread, butter beans, and home-grown sliced tomatoes. For dessert, she served "Earthquake Cake," a delectable accumulation of nuts, coconut, German chocolate cake, butter, cream cheese, and confectioner's sugar, baked earlier.

Monday morning, Lib and Annie, in her housecoat and bare feet on the concrete driveway, watched as Richard directed Paul as he backed our motorhome out of the driveway onto the street. I photographed the effort. After final thank-yous and good-byes, we drove away, waving to our new friends, Annie and Richard Carroll.

This would be a longer, more complicated day of navigating—344 miles to a campground in Georgia—than our previous travel day. For once, we got underway 10 minutes ahead of our planned departure time of eight o'clock.

During our hiatus from the road, I had relaxed from my navi-gation mode and did not think to ask what routes or campground

John and Paul had planned for that day. Nor, I discovered later, had Paul written down the route numbers. So as the morning sun cast long shadows from tall pine trees across two-lane paved roads, Paul and I blithely followed the Graybeals across various state routes in the panhandle of Florida to I-10E.

Since these routes did not have designated rest areas, when John noticed a place for one vehicle to pull over beside a cemetery, we stopped. John said he would wait for us up ahead at State Route 20. After our rest stop, we drove until we saw John ahead and Paul told him on the CB that we had him in sight. John spotted us and pulled out of his parking place and continued to lead the way.

As we headed on I-10E for Tallahassee, I turned my watch ahead an hour when I looked at the map and saw that we had come from the central time zone into the eastern time zone—an hour "lost." I thought of Lib, who had not changed her watch the whole trip. She was now in tune with the time.

Soon we turned north and entered Georgia. A roadside sign implored "Let's Keep Georgia Peachy Clean."

By noon, we had seen our first Georgia cotton field. We passed a large cotton gin with truckload-size bales of cotton stacked outside, beautiful pecan groves, and more cotton fields looking as if a light snow had fallen.

On the CB, John told Paul that we could eat lunch and refuel at Valdosta, a city about 12 miles ahead. Richard Carroll had informed John that Georgia offered the cheapest gasoline in the nation. Paul later found that the state has the lowest fuel tax in the United States.

After refueling in Valdosta, we found a Sam's Club parking lot on Norman Drive, where we ate lunch in our motorhomes. We continued on U.S. 84, a smooth, pleasant road, through the countryside and occasional towns to Waycross, Georgia. It was here that we lost contact with our leader. While we continued northeast on U.S. 84, which angled up to the northeast, to reach I-95, the Graybeals turned right onto U.S. 82, which went due east, to reach I-95. Unknowingly, we were driving miles and miles farther apart from one another. Our last contact was at 3:08 P.M., when Paul told John on the CB that we had to wait for the passing "choo-choo."

The caboose finally passed, and we continued on U.S. 84, unable to see the Graybeals, who had taken U.S. 82 out of Waycross. Hurrying to catch up, we tried to reach them on the CB.

Paul mentioned that our stop for that evening would be the Savannah South KOA Kampground at Richmond Hill, Georgia. Surely we would catch up with our friends before reaching the campground, I thought. I figured we would get to Richmond Hill about 6:15 P.M. or so.

We kept thinking they were up ahead—perhaps not too far—but Paul gave up trying to catch up. We concentrated on finding our way and being alert for the campground. A lot of noise came on the CB, but nothing sounded like John's voice.

In Flemington, Georgia, U.S. 84 makes a right angle as it heads to I-95, perhaps 10 miles east. We cruised the dual highway, listening to the CB and looking for billboards for the Savannah South KOA Kampground and for a highway sign that would point us to I-95 North.

A white egret stood as still as a statue in water beside busy highway U.S. 84 as it ended and we gained I-95 North. From the campground directory, we learned that we needed to take Exit 87 from I-95. We had not yet seen or heard from the Graybeals. Paul tried again on the CB. No response.

Paul announced the mile markers that counted upward—"81, 82, 83." Soon the KOA entrance welcomed us. We drove through tall trees to the office. There was no sign of the Graybeals.

At 5:17 P.M., Paul entered the KOA office to see what he could find out. I wondered what we would do if the Graybeals weren't there.

Paul returned from the office, laid the campground diagram on the dash, got behind the wheel, and began to move the motorhome forward. He said the office staff did not remember registering anyone named Graybeal.

I turned on the cell phone, but I didn't know if John and Lib had our cell phone number. It was 5:41 P.M. as Paul hooked up to utilities.

Twenty minutes went by as I kept an eye out the windows. Then at last I saw a familiar Southwind drive toward us and pull into the site next door.

John said that after the train at Waycross separated us, they tried to call us on the CB. They had stopped alongside the road to wait. They had even unhooked the car and John drove back several miles to see if we had a problem. Not finding us, they went on to the KOA, where we had already arrived. Lib said they figured that if we missed one another we could always find our way back to Maryland.

What did Paul and I learn? To *write down* the route numbers for that day's travel when in a caravan. Be sure your fellow travelers have your cell phone number and you have theirs. If you get separated from one another and lose contact by CB, you can try calling on the cell phone. I learned to take more responsibility for finding out our route when planning it with others.

The next day, Tuesday, we crossed the calm, wide, Savannah River with a bright blaze of sun reflecting from it at one glorious spot.

And then South Carolina welcomed us with red blooming cannas and pretty white, purple, and cranberry cosmos in the I-95 median strip. Although the main lobby of the South Carolina

Welcome Center was not open when we stopped, I picked up state maps from inside one of the open vestibules. It was hard to realize that we were headed north toward home. I felt as if we were simply traveling to another destination on our trip.

Around noon we drove into the North Carolina Welcome Center, where I visited the lobby for booklets and maps. In the parking lot, we ate lunch in our motorhomes.

Fields of cotton, soybeans, and potatoes lay alongside I-95 in North Carolina. Cattle and horses grazed in pastures. Shades of red appeared among the muted colors of tree leaves and bushes along the highway.

At Selma, North Carolina, we registered at the Lakeview KOA Kampground campground. It was our last night on the road.

The next morning we began the final leg of this journey. The Southwind and tow car plowed into the mist ahead of us in the right lane of the dual highway. The Endeavor pushed forward against a sudden wind. A van passed both of us. The headlights of oncoming traffic shone from across the median strip. As I looked ahead from the passenger seat, I mused that the highway represented time—coming to meet us was future time, where our wheels touched it was the present, and the flat surface behind us was time past.

About eleven o'clock near Petersburg, Virginia, John came on the CB: "Milkweed, do you have a copy?"

"Yes, I do," said Paul.

"We're staying on 95—295 is the bypass," John informed us. We weren't taking any chances of being separated again.

We drove through the industrial suburbs of Richmond along with multitudes of semi tractor-trailers in three lanes. Ahead were the skyscrapers of Richmond in the misty, overcast skies. We crossed the James River. We hadn't driven in traffic that heavy for quite some time. I held my breath as Paul steered the motorhome in the right lane with trucks and cars passing in the other two lanes.

About noon, we stopped at a rest area at Mile Marker 108 off I-95. It was our final stop before reaching our home. After lunch in our motorhomes, Paul asked a security officer to take a picture of the four of us—our last of the trip.

A fine mist kissed the windshield as we drove past Fredericksburg, Virginia. "I wonder what the weather is like at home—whether it's raining," I said to Paul. We mostly rode along in silence.

We passed Aquia Pines Camp Resort, which the Carrolls formerly owned. I was glad to catch a glimpse of it and to think of Richard and Annie and the good fun we had together.

Past Washington, we headed to Rockville, Maryland, as cars darted in and out of lanes like jackrabbits.

At 2:23 P.M., we took Exit 16 off I-270 and got on SR 27 toward our hometown of Westminster, Maryland. My heart reached out to the familiar rolling hills, farms nestled among them, trim brick churches, and brilliant fall leaves under a blue sky with white billowing clouds. Orange pumpkins in a patch and more in a field beckoned. Fields of dried cornstalks reminded me of my own early farm days. I felt blessed to live in Maryland.

We entered our native Carroll County. I nodded at a familiar red barn and shed on the left. White fences lined pastures for grazing horses. The sun had come out—a beautiful day in October.

I smiled as I thought of being close to home, although I had some regrets about leaving the open road. Then, a little after three o'clock, by CB we thanked the Graybeals for their company during the trip and drove our separate ways.

I savored those last moments on the road. I saw familiar scenes—Meadow Branch Church of the Brethren, the cemetery, Roop's Mill, and Woodward's meadow with cattle and donkeys. I saw them in the light of having been all across the country. They welcomed me just by being there.

We backed into our driveway, rocking across the drains, and stopped. From behind the wheel, Paul said, "Dear Lord, thank you for every safe mile." He looked at the odometer as was our custom and said, "7,992." I looked at my watch: 3:18 P.M.

Paul stayed seated in the driver's seat and leaned forward with his arms curved around the steering wheel before turning off the ignition. "Oh, I'm so grateful, and I mean *grateful*. I learned so many things this trip. It was an excellent trip. Except for that one incident early on, I think this thing behaved *excellent*," Paul summed up.

16

Maintaining and Storing Your RV after a Trip

EVENTUALLY, MOST of us go to someplace we call home. It's a place to regroup and reflect on what we learned on the road. Yet once we arrive home, there are still RV maintenance tasks that need to be done. Here are suggestions to help you.

❑ At the end of each trip, pour two ounces of chlorine bleach down each drain and flush with water to retard bacteria and keep odors down.

—Herb and Mary-Lou Pletcher (HP and M-LP), Taneytown, MD

❑ Baking soda can be poured down drains to sweeten them.

—HP and M-LP

❑ Rubber molding covers screwheads on an RV's outside seams. Water can collect beneath it and become stagnant, and mold can form. To clean the molding, remove it and soak it overnight in a chlorine bleach solution. (Use a 5-gallon bucket filled three-quarters full with water and add 1 pint of bleach—or more if mold is excessive.) Wash the area where the rubber molding was removed with the bleach solution. This kills the fungus that causes the mold. Also you can wipe the molding with a rag dipped in acetone. Acetone should be used carefully as it is highly volatile.

—Carroll and Joyce Dell, Littlestown, PA

❏ If you normally keep plants in your RV, remove them whenever you plan not to use your RV for a while. Plants cannot tolerate the extreme high and low temperatures that might occur in a vehicle out of operation.

—Professor Thomas C. Weiler, Department of Horticulture, Cornell University, NY

❏ Put mothballs in a metal (nonflammable) jar lid and place inside the water heater door (away from the main burner). This will deter spiders from nesting and/or laying eggs.

—Pete Jones, Westminster, MD

❏ When your unit is in storage, moth crystals in an open small jar placed in outside access compartments to the heater and refrigerator help keep spiders from building nests in the gas nozzles (jets). Always remember to remove the jars before activating the appliances—the crystals are flammable.

—Shirley and Jack Lippy, Westminster, MD

❏ To winterize your RV: (1) blow out your RV's water system, add RV antifreeze, and open and drain the water pump and water heater; (2) make sure the batteries are fully charged or remove them; (3) change the engine oil and filter; (4) clean and seal the roof as needed; (5) run the auxiliary power generator until the carburetor is dry of gasoline, then change the generator oil and filter.

—Elmer "Butch" Bitzer, Reichart's Camping Center, Hanover, PA

❏ If you cover your RV, protect the cover from sharp corners by adding suitable padding at those places. Tighten the cover tie-downs so as not to put excessive strain on the tie-down eyelets, which will cause them to tear away from the materials around them.

❏ Every so often disconnect the battery terminals and clean them. Corroded battery terminals can keep your engine from starting or operating properly.

❏ Sometime on the trip home, it's time to start your "To Do" list of tasks for when you get home. The list will keep you focused and prevent you from trying to do everything at once. At the top of the list should come calls to friends and family to let them know you are home safely. The laundry will wait.

❏ Unloading the RV will be easier if you organize as much as possible before you get home. The last morning on the road, change the sheets on the bed and gather towels and other laundry in a big plastic trash bag. Fill plastic grocery bags with newspapers, trip brochures, cosmetics, and audiotapes so these and other loose items will be ready to carry into the house.

❏ Sometimes after a long period of disuse, an RV's furnace won't start because its microprocessor board needs to be reset. Try removing the fuse for the microprocessor board for at least 60 seconds and then reinserting it. The location of the fuse panel varies with each manufacturer. It could be either inside the vehicle or outside in a compartment. If you can't find your fuse panel, ask a knowledgeable friend or your RV dealer. The most common types of fuses are cartridge, blade, and miniblade styles.

❏ If you haven't used your motorhome for a month or so, take it out for a drive so the fluid and lubricating systems reach their normal operating parameters as shown in the owner's manual.

❏ To keep the refrigerator smelling clean while the RV is not being used, fill an old stocking with charcoal and leave it in the unit. Put one in the freezer compartment too.

———— ◇ ————

Unpacking

FOR SIX WEEKS, I hadn't thought much about our homecoming. Our last night out, I asked Lib how she was going to handle getting home and wanting to do everything at once. She replied, "John says we will just take one day at a time and do what we can." That sounded calming to me. I made a mental note to myself that if I had something distasteful to do, I would start it and not think about getting it done. The idea behind that was as long as I can *start* a project, I will eventually wind up finishing it, and it's not as stressful to think about starting something as it is to think about finishing the whole job at once.

When we arrived home from our 44-day trek, I started doing the tasks on my homecoming checklist.

First, I phoned Nancy, our daughter-in-law, to say we were safely home. Then I got our phone messages and replied, checked for faxes and dealt with them immediately. I called the *Times* to restart the newspaper and the post office to change mail delivery to us from Jeff, our son. When Paul brought in my laptop, I hooked it up and looked at my e-mail.

Paul brought in the food from the motorhome and then other items. I did a load of white laundry. After Paul and I ate frozen entrées for dinner, I finished the travel log and totals. Then I folded and put away the laundry, took a shower, and went to bed.

The next day I was up at 6:11 A.M. and began working in an unhurried mode, determined to complete jobs as I came to them. We brought in our clothes and finished unloading at our own pace.

Eventually, with the weather turning cold and no plans to use the motorhome during the winter, Paul began to winterize the coach. He filled the fuel tank to prevent condensation, changed the motor oil and motor oil filter for the diesel engine, and drained the water from the fuel/water separator to prevent its freezing and causing a problem. He checked that the tires were properly inflated and placed wheel covers over those on the sunny side of the motorhome. He removed the water from the plumbing system and put in a special antifreeze. Last of all, together we put a new gray lightweight tarpaulin over the entire coach to protect it from the winter weather.

Paul always has ongoing projects for the motorhome. He's planning to add cupboards above the entry door and overhead beside the driver's seat. He dreams of building a wood cabinet with pullout drawers that will fit into one of the basement compartments. It will hold his tools and make them easily accessible.

He also likes to make small adjustments that make a big difference in comforts. One of these is moving the clothes rod in the wardrobe of the coach toward the rear only a half-inch—just enough to make it easier to close the sliding mirrored doors without catching sleeves in it. We love that spacious wardrobe and its location in the bathroom area, which offers an unusually large amount of dressing room.

The Alaskan caravaner reunion certainly did not turn out the way we expected. Would we have gone had we known before we left home that Clem was in the hospital and Effie would need to be near him? We probably would have done what Effie wanted us to do: go to the campgrounds that she had already reserved and paid a nonrefundable deposit on. It was admirable of Effie and Clem to invite us for a reunion in the first place. They spent a lot of time and effort planning it and they could be proud that it went as well as it could have without them.

We appreciated the fact that all the caravaners rallied to make the best of a disappointing situation: Effie provided lunch and information and materials for us, the Cornells drove the unfamiliar motorhome of the Swagertys and then stayed in an unheated cabin in order to be with us, and the Wrigleys and the Graybeals hosted us in their motorhomes for hors d'oeuvres and ice cream parties. While we agreed that it would be better in the future to get together regionally, we were glad that we had this one last fling.

By November, a note from Effie said that Clem was recovering well. Although his legs hurt and he walked with two canes, he could drive the car short distances.

I still feel so indebted to our friends and fellow travelers, Lib and John, for staying with us when we had our engine trouble at the beginning of our journey. They could have driven on to Osage Beach and played golf on one of the many attractive courses there. Instead, they helped us in more ways than we can say.

As he did on our trip to Colorado, Paul drove all the way on this trip to California. (Actually, I drove perhaps 50 feet in campground entrance driveways.) I want to do more driving when just the two of us are on a trip, preferably on a dual highway. Also, I want to learn more about driving a diesel so that I will have more confidence in the driver's seat. In fact, I plan to attend an RV driving school (see the appendix).

It was great to be back in Maryland, with its familiar towns and landscape. The colored leaves were truly beautiful in the sunshine. I'm glad we did not miss seeing their deep reds against the bright golds and vibrant greens.

While we tucked our motorhome cozily under a gray tarpaulin for the winter, we plan to take it out of hibernation in the spring. Meanwhile, we'll have dreams of where to roam next. Perhaps to Savannah or Prince Edward Island or even Alaska again or who knows where?

17

Traveling with Children and Pets

ALTHOUGH OUR motorhome usually contains just the two of us, many people take their children or grandchildren along for the ride. Traveling by RV is more economical for families than flying and staying in hotels, and taking children camping enriches the whole family. Pets like to go along too. This chapter will show you how to make the trip more enjoyable for everyone.

Traveling with Children

❑ To keep children involved and interested on a long road trip, refer to a map of your itinerary and list all the towns, cities, counties, and points of interest and use it as a geographic treasure map. The children check off each site as they travel through it. They could also use a highlighter pen to trace the trip on their own map, circling stops and points of interest.

—Jack and Shirley Lippy, Westminster, MD

❑ Keeping a rug or old piece of carpet outside the door helps minimize the amount of dirt carried inside on everyone's feet. Better yet, leave your shoes at the door.

—Charlene Schweikhart, Indianapolis, IN

❑ Take along a little portable swimming pool for the children to enjoy in camp on those hot days.

—Kathleen Bailey (KB), Westminster, MD

❑ Many campgrounds have special weekend events for children during the summer. Campgrounds where you've stayed before may send you a calendar, or try searching the Internet for campground Web sites. Start planning in early spring so you won't miss out on the fun.

—KB

❑ Overpack when it comes to toys and games that will keep everyone busy and happy.

—KB

❑ Even on the road, your children and their young guests should have certain duties to be responsible for. Such tasks help each person feel like part of the group.

—Fran Lathe (FL), Westminster, MD

❑ We feel that our teenagers are safer in most campgrounds than they would be in a hotel or motel. We can let them roam a bit on their own. Family communicators keep everyone in touch and round up the kids from wherever they are in the campground. We make sure they know the campground rules, especially about safety and noise.

—FL

❑ If your RV is usually overflowing with extra children— friends or cousins along for the trip—bring along a tent for them to camp in beside the RV.

—FL

❑ Bring plenty of items that will keep your children active after a long day on the road—sports gear, snorkels, bikes.

At a campground, two people throwing a football around can soon become a full-fledged touch football game.

—FL

❑ Pay attention to the campground rules and explain them to your children. Most of the time they are there for the children's safety. Don't be one of those parents who turn their little ones loose to annoy other campers or get into dangerous situations.

—FL

❑ When camping with children in a pop-up trailer or other vehicle that does not have a bathroom, experienced parents choose a campsite close to a campground restroom.

—FL

❑ Using a sleeping bag for children at bedtime eliminates making up a bed with sheets and blankets, and the children like it because it seems more like camping. Simply roll up the sleeping bag in the morning.

—Joyce and Carroll Dell (JD and CD), Littlestown, PA

❑ When you camp with children or grandchildren, keep the following items on hand to entertain them if the weather is bad: games, puzzles, videos, coloring books and crayons, and snacks such as popsicles, juice, and pretzels. Outside items (for when the weather is good) can include any throwing game, such as a Frisbee or a Velcro ball and catch mitt, which keeps the children busy in the campsite without bothering neighboring campers.

—JD and CD

❑ If you camp in national parks during the summer, take advantage of the many free ranger-led activities offered by the National Park Service, such as campfires, nature hikes, and informative talks. You may find a few activities offered in the off-season as well.

❑ Keep a small whisk broom handy near the entry so your family can brush dirt or sand off their shoes and clothes before they enter the RV.

❑ Take food that everyone likes, but be prepared to eat out too.

❑ Pack After Bite in your first aid or toiletries kit. It really works to stop the itch of mosquito bites. It comes in a small lipstick-sized tube with a screw top.

❑ Bring along a few birthday napkins and candles if someone in your family will be celebrating a birthday on the road. (Parents appreciate a little festivity on their special days too.)

❑ Involve the whole family in "departure" meetings so every-one knows the day's plans and destinations and routes.

Traveling with Pets

❑ If traveling with dogs, it's important to obedience train them, control them, and clean up after them immediately. Teach your dog to stay alone without barking (unless someone is trying to get into the RV). If you can't train on your own, find a group through a veterinarian, kennels, or the yellow pages, and don't give up. Patience, persis-tence, and practice will pay off. You won't believe the compliments you'll get on your dog's manners.
—Lt. Col. Virginia Dillon (VD), Alexandria, VA

❑ If you plan to visit a state or national park with your pet, check to see what the rules are before you go. If dogs are allowed, you must have them on a leash at all times. Be aware that a lot of parks and campgrounds will not let you tie your dog outside. Some major attractions, such as Carlsbad Caverns in New Mexico and most of the Disney parks, have kennels where your pet can spend the day while you visit the attraction.

—VD

❑ Don't give your pets too much water or food before you get on the road. Carry your pets' current identification and be sure you have clean-up equipment. (Your neighbors will thank you.) Take a swivel stake for tying your pet and a square of linoleum or carpet to place under food and water dishes.

—Herb and Mary-Lou Pletcher, Taneytown, MD

❑ An RV can be the ideal way to travel with any pet. Nevertheless, some animals travel better than others. Only you know your pet's personality well enough to decide whether bringing him or her along is a good idea. The best travelers are confident and accustomed to change and trustworthy around strangers.

—Cynthia D. Miller (CM), Yuba City, CA

❑ Your pet will need a travel checklist too, so you won't forget to pack everything he or she needs for a comfortable trip: food and treats, medicine, bedding, grooming necessities, collar and leash, pooper scooper, food and water dishes, and toys.

—CM

❑ When traveling with a dog, you must plan to stop every hour or two for at least 10 minutes. Highway rest areas provide grassy plots for caretakers to walk their pets.

—CM

❑ Ask your veterinarian what paperwork you need if you will be crossing state lines or over the border to Canada or Mexico. No matter where you're going, you should bring along a copy of a current health certificate, immunization records, and rabies certificate for your dog. Rabies tags are not always enough proof. Each state has different rules about what is considered a "current" health certificate, so check what the rules are in each state where you'll be stopping.
—CM

❑ Have your pet wear a collar with a securely attached identification tag at all times on your trip. The tag should list the telephone number of a friend, relative, or veterinarian at home plus the number of your cellular telephone, if you're bringing one along.
—CM

❑ Before you leave home, prepare a small card listing important phone numbers. You'll need numbers for your veterinarian, the American Animal Hospital Association Veterinary Emergency Information (800-252-2242), the Humane Society's Lost Pet Hotline (900-535-1515), and the National Animal Poison Control Center. Have the card laminated (or do it yourself) and carry it with you at all times.
—CM

❑ Before you travel with your pet,
- Take your pet to the veterinarian for a physical exam and update on all vaccines. Most vaccines are updated yearly.
- Tell your veterinarian where you plan on traveling. Your veterinarian may recommend specific medications or

vaccines depending on your destination. For example, mosquitoes in many regions of the country (and North and South America) carry a heartworm parasite, which can cause heart disease in dogs. Giving a monthly medication during mosquito season can prevent heartworm infection. Your veterinarian may also recommend that your dog receive a vaccination against Lyme disease, which is spread by ticks in certain regions of the country.

- If you plan to cross an international border, request a health certificate and proof of rabies vaccination from your veterinarian. Generally, health certificates must be signed within 30 days of travel.

- If your pet takes medication regularly, remember to get a supply that will carry you through the whole length of your trip. This same recommendation is true if your pet requires a special diet.

- Obtain a copy of your pet's health and vaccination record. This information may be helpful if you have to visit a veterinarian while you are on the road. In addition, if you have to kennel your pet while you are on the road, you will need to provide proof of vaccination before most kennels will accept your pet.

- If your pet is not accustomed to travel, take it for a few short rides before setting out on a long trip.

- Update your pet's identification information (tags). In addition, it is now possible to have your veterinarian implant a small microchip under your dog's or cat's skin. The information from the microchip is reported to a national registry that shelters can contact to reunite lost pets with their owners. Most shelters now routinely scan all pets for microchip identification when they first arrive.

While on the road with your pet,

- Use caution when leaving your pet unattended in a vehicle. The temperature in parked vehicles can climb quickly and endanger or kill your pet. Lock all doors and open enough windows to provide adequate ventilation. If the windows are not screened, remember to limit the opening so your pet cannot jump out or get its head stuck. In warm weather, ensure that the air conditioner is functioning and that there is constant access to a fresh supply of cool water.

- Traveling and unfamiliar settings may cause your pet to become nervous, and familiar objects may help reduce anxiety. Remember to bring your pet's favorite bed, toys, and dishes.

- Try to stick to your regular feeding routine whenever possible. When traveling, give the main meal at the end of the day or after you have reached your final destination.

- At campgrounds, keep your pet on a leash and in sight at all times. In rural areas, skunks, snakes, coyotes, raccoons, and even other camper's animals can bite or injure your pet.

- Consider traveling with a kennel to contain your pet at campgrounds and at other times when you don't want it roaming around the RV.

  —Guy Mulder, DVM, Director, University Laboratory Animal Resources, University of California, Irvine

—————— ⟨⟩ ——————

RVing Today

A RECENT STUDY by the University of Michigan Survey Research Center shows that more RVs are owned by families with children than by over-55 empty nesters. After we returned to Maryland, I talked with two mothers who shared their RVing stories and insights.

The first was Kathleen K. Bailey, a certified public accountant who works from her home office outside of Westminster, Maryland. Her husband, John, works in a computer programming center. They have two daughters, Kaitlyn, 6, and Kristina, 3. Their RV, which Kathleen refers to as the "camper," is a Type C Rockwood motorhome, 18 feet in length, with a Dodge motor. They have owned it for about four years.

When I asked Kathleen what made them decide to get into RVing, she chuckled: "One afternoon, we needed to make some plans for a quick weekend outing. I said to my husband, 'Why don't you ask your dad if we can borrow his camper?'" He had purchased it from a neighbor and it had been sitting in his driveway for a couple of years.

John's dad readily agreed. So they took the Rockwood motorhome to Granite Hill Campground, Gettysburg, for the weekend. They loved the experience. John returned the camper to his parents, who lived about 40 miles away.

The next weekend, they decided to borrow the camper again. After another great weekend, John's dad said that they didn't have to bring the camper back because they had used it more than anybody. It was theirs to keep. They had become instant RV owners.

While John enjoys traveling in the RV, his zest does not equal that of Kathleen and the girls. The three of them often take the camper on a Friday night and spend the night away from home. "Girls night out," Kathleen calls it.

A favorite place for the whole family to go is Dutch Wonderland, an amusement park in Pennsylvania. Adjacent is the Old Mill Stream campground, a very clean and friendly place. When the children (or their parents) get tired or hungry during the day, they just go next door to their camper to rest or have lunch.

Surprisingly, when I asked Kathleen what she liked most about RVing, she said she liked to cook in the RV! "And we don't cook just normal food," Kathleen laughed. "We cook food with enticing aromas like bacon or fried chicken—something that just drives people crazy when they go past the camper."

When they travel, the children ride in the Ford Expedition SUV with Kathleen. They follow John, who drives the camper. The children used to ride in the camper, but once when John had to brake hard, Kaitlyn hit her head hard on the table, even though she was wearing her seat belt. When their present RV goes to "camper heaven," they plan to buy a towable and pull it with the Expedition.

Because there are periods when she and John are setting up the camper or putting items away, Kathleen needs to keep the girls happy and occupied. Thus, the camper is full of games and toys.

When I asked Kathleen how often she camped, she answered, "Not often enough." About March, she starts thumbing through campground calendars, which list activities and special events for the weekends each summer. She obtains campground calendars from being on the mailing list of places where she has stayed. She also gets information from the Internet.

Every year, she tries to fit into their calendar Dutch Wonderland in Lancaster, Granite Hill Campground in Gettysburg, and Yogi Bear's Jellystone Park in Lancaster. She tries to go to campgrounds that have fun events for the children.

An accountant, Kathleen has created a spreadsheet that makes getting ready for a camping excursion quicker. It includes menus with lists of foods needed and makes grocery shopping easier. It acts as a checklist and a To Do list.

While the Baileys sometimes camp by themselves, they like to go with another family because they have not been RVing long enough to know what to do when something in the camper breaks.

Fran Lathe, a friend and neighbor of Kathleen's who goes RVing, also shared her story with me.

Fran and Larry Lathe, both 43, own LML Remodeling, Inc., Westminster, Maryland. They have two children: Joe, 15, and Samantha, 13. They own a 39-foot Holiday Rambler Imperial diesel pusher with a slideout in the rear bedroom and another in the living area.

Fran and Larry started out with a tent about 15 years ago. They progressed to a pop-up towable, a conversion van, and a previously owned motorhome before buying the new motorhome. When they were in between campers, they stayed in hotels and motels but found they preferred to know who had slept in the bed last.

Another reason they bought the RV is that their business has never slowed down from the first day, and the only way they can get away from it is to "hop in that thing and take off. And then we just check the messages when we get back," Fran said.

They continue RVing because they feel their teenagers are safe in most campgrounds; they can let them roam without having to keep constant watch. In motels or hotels, Fran would not let the children out the door without a parent. They have small radio communicators to summon the youth home when needed from wherever they are in the campground. While participating in the many activities available at the campground, the teens check into the camper from time to time. They have some freedom and their parents don't worry about them.

"We never travel, especially locally, with just our own kids. There's always a nephew going along, or a cousin, or somebody else's kids. And we just stick them in a tent outside if there's not enough room inside. With the slideout, there's plenty of room to set up the air mattress on the floor if we need to," said Fran.

The Lathes also travel with a German shepherd, Nyla, and two cockatiels. (The dog will misbehave if she is left behind.) When Fran loads the coach, Nyla stays by her side, ready to start another adventure.

As for the cockatiels, when Fran goes away for a night or two, she will leave them at home. But if the Lathes are gone longer, Fran puts the birds in a smaller cage and sets it on the floor of the coach when they are going down the road. When they park at a campground, Fran tilts the steering wheel so that it lies flat. She places a round wood disk on top, covers it with a tablecloth, and sets the cage with the cockatiels on top of it.

Round Top Campground, Gettysburg, Pennsylvania, is at the top of Fran's campground list because of the relationships the family has formed there and the activities offered. When the Lathes first camped there, the new owners faced major repairs of the facilities and grounds. They had a special fix-up weekend at the opening of the camping season. Fran and Larry went to help. Instead of raking leaves, they offered their carpentry skills and helped put together one of the bathrooms. Since then, they have become friends with the owners. Their children have become friends with other campers' children. The family likes to explore the nearby Gettysburg battlefields as well as participate in activities at the campground itself.

To make it enjoyable to camp with children, Fran likes to find campgrounds that offer special activities for the holidays. Many campgrounds celebrate Halloween on two weekends because people like to decorate their campsites, participate in all kinds of contests, like pumpkin carving, and go trick-or-treating.

Fran has even celebrated Thanksgiving in the RV. She cooked the turkey and carved it before leaving home and then they enjoyed a turkey dinner in the motorhome.

When traveling down the road, the children can watch a video or take a nap or play games. They can take advantage of the restroom facilities, refrigerator, and pantry without having to stop.

Since Paul and I had a diesel engine in our new motorhome, which I had not yet mastered, I asked Fran if she knew how to operate their new diesel motorhome. Matter of factly, she said Larry's work truck was a diesel and she had driven another truck that was diesel, so they were used to that type of engine.

"It's a lot easier than most people think, but you still have to be conscious that you are driving something the size of a passenger bus," Fran said.

Sometimes the Lathes camp with their neighbors who also have an RV. Many times, although they travel together on the road and stay at the same place, the families end up participating in different activities and do not see much of one another.

Camping brings families closer, Fran said. The confined space means that people talk to one another, figure out what other people want to do, and learn the interests and personalities of one another. She thinks she and Larry know their teenagers better because they spend more time with them as they travel in the motorhome.

"When you're in the camper or around the campsite, you end up talking about things that you probably wouldn't have time for if you were at home," Fran said.

They are not strict disciplinarians, Fran said, but they do expect certain duties to be done, even by young guests, when they get to a campsite. The children may not go to the store or play until the picnic table is moved to a suitable place, the bikes are unloaded, and other tasks are done. These tasks turn out to be fun at a campground. In addition, Fran said such work helps each person feel like a part of the group.

Once the weather warms up in the spring, Fran starts to stock the food pantry in the motorhome. When she buys canned goods for the house, she buys extras and puts them in the motorhome. If her family decides at the last minute to take off for a weekend, Fran said that almost all campgrounds are located near grocery stores.

Fran said that she and Larry will work hard to see that their children get a college education, but at this stage in their lives, the children are also getting an education by going places and sharing experiences with their parents. Realizing that many people become unable to travel after retiring, they decided to purchase their "retirement motorhome" while they could enjoy it.

Fran summed up her feelings: "Too many people just wait and say, 'Well, we'll do this once the kids grow up.' We're doing it now. My parents were the same way. I have been to every state except Alaska. My parents didn't have a lot of money, but we were able to visit all of those places because we had a camper when I was a kid. Now we're doing the same thing with our children."

In case you think that RVing is expensive, a study by PKF Consulting, an independent research firm, showed that traveling by RV costs less than a cruise; an all-inclusive air/hotel/meal package; a trip involving air travel, rental cars, restaurants and hotels; and travel to a condo or rental property by personal car or airline. Traveling by RV was 13 to 42 percent lower in cost than driving in a personal car, staying in hotels, and eating in restaurants.

Lest you think that all RVers are in excellent health, thousands of people with special needs become mobile and have fun in an RV on the road. Special-needs RVs and conversion vans are outfitted with features that make it possible for people with mobility concerns by some 15 manufacturers. These include wheelchair lifts or ramps, lower kitchen counters and cabinets, widened entrances to roll-in showers, and other features.

Millions of people are realizing and enjoying the many advantages of travel by RV. One University of Michigan Survey Research Center study said that households owning RVs number 8.6 million and that figure is expected to grow to 10.4 million in the year 2010. More than 45 percent of these owners are between the ages of 35 and 54 (compared to 40 percent ages 55 and older).

The RVing image today shows people of all ages, robust or with special needs, in many types of recreational vehicles that suit their budgets, on the road for a weekend, a vacation span, an extended tour, or full time. It's a smart, economical, enjoyable way to travel.

The destinations and excitement of traveling in a recreational vehicle are endless. And, as you probably know, the people who travel in RVs are some of the most generous and helpful folks you'll ever meet. I'm grateful to all the experienced RVers who suggested tips for this book. I hope you'll consider contributing a tip or two of your own. You can fax your tips to me at 410-857-3835, or mail them to Tips for RVing, Arbor House Publishing, 332-140 Village Road #7-197, Westminster, MD 21157. Please be sure to include your name, address, and phone number.

Meanwhile, my best wishes to you in the fulfillment of your dreams. I hope that we see you on your travels.

Appendix

FOR ADDITIONAL information on RV travel, you may refer to the following sections in this appendix:

Restaurants
Rest Areas, Picnic Areas, and Welcome Centers
Recipes
Recommended Campgrounds
Places of Interest
Campground and Truck Center Directories
Membership Benefit Cards
Publications
Travelers with Special Needs
Driving Schools
RV Trade Associations
Trip Statistics
Travel Checklist
Itinerary

Restaurants

Should you travel to the locations along the routes in this book, you may choose to seek out the following restaurants. Their food pleased our palates.

The Golden Lamb, 27 South Broadway, Lebanon, OH 45036, 513-932-5065. Casual dress, children's menu. Dining room is in a historic inn, well preserved. Varied menu, including lamb. Interesting, pleasant atmosphere, excellent service, and good food. After dinner, we enjoyed touring the upstairs, which has 18 guest rooms named for famous visitors, such as 10 U.S. Presidents and 19th century literary figures Charles Dickens, Mark Twain, and Harriet Beecher Stowe.

Cracker Barrel Old Country Store, at Exit 19 off I-71 near Kings Island, Cincinnati, OH. A dependable source of good, family-style food in an informal rustic setting with friendly service.

Richards Farm Restaurant, 607 NE 13th Street, Casey, IL 62420, 217-932-5300, fax 217-932-4097. The owners renovated a barn into a restaurant and kept its rustic appearance. Full menu offers entrées with pork, beef, seafood, and chicken plus soup, salad, and bread bar. Casual dress, children's menu. Excellent food.

Kenilworth Restaurants, 3245 Bagnell Dam Boulevard, Lake Ozark, MO 65049, 573-365-2300. A bakery with wide selection of pastries associated with the restaurant.

Country Kitchen, Highway 54, ½ mile west of Grand Glaize Bridge, Osage Beach, MO 65049, 573-348-4554. Family style, full menu with senior and children's menus, clean modern dining area, good food.

Kirby House Restaurant, 205 N.E. Third, Abilene, KS 67410, 785-263-7336, fax 785-263-1885, www.kirby-house.com. Casual dining in restored Victorian house, children's menu, excellent service and food. This is Paul's favorite place to find delicious, tender steak. Their desserts are outstanding also.

The Irma Hotel, 1192 Sheridan Avenue, Cody, WY 82414, 307-587-4221. Dining room is on the first floor of hotel built by Buffalo Bill Cody. Live music. Casual wear. Full menu plus soup and salad bar. No reservations unless staying in the hotel. May have a short wait. Good service and food. I loved its real Western atmosphere.

Wagon Wheel Restaurant, 435 N. Cache, Jackson, WY 83001, 307-733-2492. Casual wear. Closed during October and November. Western atmosphere with photograph of the Grand Tetons by Ansel Adams. Good food and service.

The Fishwife Seafood Café, 789 Trinity, Seaside, CA 93955. Casual atmosphere, sidewalk or inside dining. Seafood was fresh and delicious. Excellent service. This restaurant is in the same building with the Turtle Bay Taqueria on the corner of Fremont Boulevard and Trinity.

Peachwood's at The Inn at Pasatiempo, 555 Highway 17, Santa Cruz, CA 95060, 408-423-5000, fax 831-426-3112, e-mail PeachwoodsSteak@aol.com. Upscale, casual dress, pleasant and relaxing dining, interesting clocks hang on the walls, reservations preferred. Delicious food well served.

One Main Street, 1 Main Street, Salinas, CA 93901, 831-775-4733. Located in the National Steinbeck Center. Sit-down service with menu of salads, sandwiches, and pastas. Reservations not necessary. Good food and friendly service.

Don Quixote Restaurant, 6275 Highway 9, Felton, CA 95018, 408-335-2800. Menu offers mostly Mexican and some American selections, casual dress. Good food.

Gillwood's Restaurant, 1320 Napa Town Center, Napa, CA 94559, 707-253-0409. Casual dining, full menu, good sandwiches and salads. Friendly service.

Lyon's Restaurant, 732 E. Washington, Petaluma, CA 94953, 707-762-4876. Casual dress, truly excellent chicken spinach salad. Children eat free every Tuesday. Friendly, prompt service.

A. Sabella's Restaurant, 2766 Taylor Street, San Francisco, CA 94133, 415-771-6775. Fine dining, casual dress, dining room is on third floor and overlooks Fisherman's Wharf. Take elevator to third floor from street level. Excellent food and service.

River House Restaurant, 222 Weller Street, Petaluma, CA 94952, 707-769-0123, www.The-River-House.com. Many dining rooms on two floors, menu varies, reservations a good idea, casual dress.

Excellent food and service. We held our farewell dinner there and had a memorable evening.

Ocean Sierra Restaurant, 3292 E. Westfall, Mariposa, CA, 95338, 209-742-7050. Located halfway between Mariposa and Oakhurst at the intersection of Triangle and E. Westfall. Serves dinner Friday through Sunday, 5–9 P.M. Selection of entrées that include soup, salad, vegetables, and bread. Known for their blueberry bread pudding and crystalized rose petals. Pleasant, wooded surroundings, excellent food and service.

Ted's Truck Center, Bull Pen Restaurants, Exit 17 off I-10, Quartzsite, AZ 85346, 520-927-5535. Truck stop restaurant, full menu and buffet, friendly fast service, good food, souvenir and accessory store.

Carver's Steakhouse, 8172 West Bell Road, Glendale, AZ 85308-8704, 623-412-0787, fax 623-412-0454. Fine dining, casual dress, reservations preferred, excellent food and service.

Rosebuds Fine Food & Drink Restaurant, 320 N. Highway 89A, Sedona, AZ 86336, 520-282-3022. Dining rooms overlook red rock monuments, casual atmosphere, pleasant house music, good food and very friendly, excellent service.

Cracker Barrel Old Country Store, 16845 North 84th Avenue, Peoria, AZ 85382, 623-875-1136. Family-style dining, full menu, excellent food and service, may have to wait a few minutes in rocking chairs on pleasant front porch, gift shop.

Old San Francisco Steak House, 10223 Sahara, San Antonio, TX 78216, 210-342-2321, fax 210-366-1623. One of five top steakhouses in Texas, unique 1800s atmosphere, live music, fun entertainment, reservations a good idea. Excellent food and service. A great place to be hosted by friends to celebrate our wedding anniversary.

My Back Porch, 1481 South Main, Boerne, TX 78006, 830-816-2782 or 830-249-2287. Casual, children's and senior plates, menu includes barbecued meats, appetizers, salads, and desserts, home-style food, buffet-style service. Good food and friendly atmosphere.

Jaspers American Eatery, 4300 Northwest Cary Parkway, Cary, NC 27513, 919-319-3400, fax 919-319-3900. Casual dress, full menu. Excellent food and friendly, prompt service. Children love to eat there too.

Rest Areas, Picnic Areas, and Welcome Centers

Like the oasis in the desert is to the nomad, so rest areas along highways are to RV and other vehicle travelers. Rest areas may or may not have restrooms: the difference is noted by a specific symbol on road maps and stated on highway signs as you approach the site. In either case, they are welcome places to pull off the road to refresh oneself. Some rest areas without restrooms are called "picnic areas" and may have small pavilions for enjoying a meal that you bring along. Some rest areas are also "welcome centers." These are located either just before crossing the border into a different state or just afterward. Some maps will have a question mark (?) symbol that indicates a welcome center. Other maps will simply note the words "Welcome Center" on the map along with the rest area symbol. Welcome centers differ in each state, but usually they offer maps, booklets, and brochures showing activities as well as places of interest and accommodations in that state. Some even offer a refreshing drink of orange juice or soda. Staff are on hand to answer questions and give options regarding your travel interests.

Besides stopping to use the restroom, many RVers use rest areas to stretch their legs, inspect their tires or the rig, chat with truck drivers or other RVers, walk the dog in the pet area, buy a newspaper, get travel answers and brochures at the information center, eat a snack or a meal, look at a map, make a call from a public telephone, or switch drivers. Some rest areas even provide dump stations and sites for overnight RV parking.

Recipes

Along our way, I collected recipes for a few dishes that were especially tasty and/or easy to prepare.

Chicken Thighs or Chicken Breasts

12 boneless, skinless chicken thighs or 8 large chicken breasts
1 package of dry onion soup (Lipton's)
1 can of cranberry sauce (with berries) or 12 oz. jar of
    apricot jam
8 oz. jar of Russian or French Dressing
Mix together last three ingredients till berries are loose. Spray Pam on bottom of the pan. Put chicken in pan. Pour mixture over. Cover with foil. Bake 45 minutes in 350-degree oven. During last 15 minutes, take foil off. Let rest 5–10 minutes out of oven.
—Mary Jo Cornell, Fairfield, CT

Ostrich Burgers

Separate frozen ostrich burgers into individual patties. Rub on both sides with olive oil. Add condiments to taste—garlic, pepper, and salt. You can barbecue or fry the patties in a skillet. In the skillet, add enough olive oil to coat the pan. Heat pan to 360 degrees. Sear burger on one side for 30 seconds. On that first side, when bubbles of blood come to the surface, turn the burger over and sear that side for 30 seconds. This will brown and seal in the juices. Then cook one and a half to two minutes on both sides. Rare to medium doneness is best. Longer cooking will dry out the meat. You can treat the ostrich burger exactly as you treat a beef burger and add gravy or onions or whatever you like. Ostrich burgers are high in protein and iron and low in fat, cholesterol, and calories.

—David Telling, Aussie's Ostriches, Merced, CA 209-238-9891, fax 209-238-9893

Microwave Rice Pudding

You can make this rice pudding in your microwave. Take 1 quart milk, ¼ cup of sugar, ¼ cup of ordinary rice (not Minute Rice), put into a large casserole bowl, and microwave without covering it for 20 minutes. Stir, cook 20 more minutes, stir again, then cook by 5-minute intervals and stir each time. It will not be thick when done but will thicken when it cools.

—Trudy Albee, Sun City, AZ

Earthquake Cake

Grease a 9x13-inch pan. Preheat oven to 350 degrees. Sprinkle 1 cup chopped nuts (I use pecans) and 1 cup coconut in bottom of pan. (I buy the canned coconut and use the whole can.)

Mix a German chocolate cake mix by the box directions and pour over the nuts and coconut. Do not use a devil's food cake mix.

Melt one stick of butter or margarine, one 8-ounce package of cream cheese, and 1 box of confectioner's sugar. Mix well. I use a wire whisk to make sure all of the sugar is melted—no lumps! Pour this mixture, while still hot, over the cake batter. Bake about 40 minutes. Check the cake at intervals so it doesn't get too brown. Very easy to prepare and serve!

—Annie Carroll, Panama City, FL

Country Grits and Sausage Casserole

2 cups water
½ tsp. salt
½ cup uncooked quick grits
4 cups extra sharp grated cheddar cheese (sold in dairy cases, already grated)

1 lb. sausage browned and drained (Jimmy Dean, regular,
    has very little fat)
4 eggs, beaten
1 cup milk
½ tsp. thyme
⅛ tsp. garlic powder

Bring water and salt to a boil, stir in grits. Return to boil, reduce heat. Cook 4 minutes. Combine grits and cheese. Stir until cheese is melted. Combine eggs, milk, thyme, and garlic to egg mixture, stirring well. Then stir egg mixture into grits mixture, adding slowly and stirring really well again. Add sausage. Add chopped green onions, canned sliced mushrooms, and chopped green chiles to the top of this mixture. Pour in a 9x13-inch baking dish, sprayed with Pam. Cover and refrigerate overnight. Let stand 15 minutes before baking at 350 degrees for 1 hour. You can make this ahead of time, put it in the freezer, take it out before going to bed, and put it in the oven the next morning. If put in the ice box while still frozen, it won't thaw out before morning. Serve this dish with crescent rolls and sliced fresh fruit. It is to die for!

—Annie Carroll, Panama City, FL

Hobo Meal

This is a meal that is cooked in the campfire. Stack a few layers of aluminum foil. Place on top of the foil the raw meat, seasonings, and raw vegetables of your choice. Fold the aluminum foil around it, seal it, and throw it gently into the campfire, being careful not to burn yourself. After several hours or when you think it is done as indicated by the burnt look of the foil, take long tongs and pull it out of the fire. Open it carefully to avoid steam burns. Family and friends serve themselves to whatever they like of the mix. Ground beef, pork, chicken, or fish can be used.

—Kathleen Bailey, Westminster, MD

Recommended Campgrounds

If you should happen to be near any of these campgrounds, I would recommend them. They all have full service hookups and welcome children and pets unless noted. They have friendly owners or staff who are oriented toward RVers. You can find the directions to the campgrounds in your favorite directory.

Wolfie's Family Kamping, Zanesville, OH. Takes long vehicles, beautiful entrance, next to nature on wooded hilltop.

Olive Branch Campground, Oregonia, OH. Peaceful, wooded country road entrance. Did not mind or charge for our early arrival. (Of course, we did not stay longer than 24 hours overall.)

Columbus Woods-N-Waters Kampground, Inc., Columbus, IN. We've stayed here several times—level, wide sites in shady grove.

Osage Beach RV Park, Osage Beach, MO. Owner was hospitable even when we arrived late at night. Campground well kept. Resort area for boating, water-skiing, fishing, golfing, amusement centers, shopping, and entertainment.

Covered Wagon Campground, Abilene, KS. Close to the Eisenhower Center and other Abilene places of interest. Owners helped me get e-mail in their office.

Camp Inn Trailer Park, Oakley, KS. Owner helped make appointment for hairdresser in nearby Oakley. Unusual garden beside swimming pool.

AB Camping, Cheyenne, WY. Nice laundry in Western deco–style building.

Ponderosa Campground, Cody, WY. Staff helped me get my e-mail in the registration office. Located just up the street from the Buffalo Bill Historical Center.

Grant Village Campground, Yellowstone National Park, WY. No hookups, but has a dump. Shower house lighted all night. In pine forest. Drive to Old Faithful in car.

The Fishing Bridge RV Park, Yellowstone National Park, WY. 340 RV sites with full hookups that cost $30.24 per night with no reduction for a Golden Eagle Passport.

Montpelier Creek KOA Kampground, Montpelier, ID. Inviting laundry room. Owner has unique communication system that definitely works for RVers to call him if office and store are closed.

Camp VIP, Salt Lake City, UT. Level, wide sites, with rows exceptionally well marked.

Hi-Desert RV Park, Winnemucca, NV. Our second stay at this park. Propane available as you park to register at the office. Paul enjoyed the swirling water in the hot tub.

Stillman Adult RV Park, Sacramento, CA. Gated park, located in Sacramento, adult oriented, 40-foot maximum vehicle length, no one under 18 may stay overnight in the park, two pets maximum per site.

Marina Dunes R.V. Park, Marina, CA. Very large game room, within walking distance of Monterey Bay. Should have reservations. About eight miles north of Monterey Peninsula.

San Francisco North/Petaluma KOA Kampground, CA. Offers van tours of San Francisco (34 miles to the south). Large laundry, shaded wide sites in country, camping cabins, petting farm, large recreation hall with kitchen facilities.

Adelanto R.V. Park & Resort, Adelanto, CA. In high desert. Park roads are wide and asphalted. Sites have concrete patios and gravel. Topnotch laundry and store.

Holiday Palms RV Park, Quartzsite, AZ. Palm trees at many sites. Cactus garden near office. Adult park—visiting children welcome under adult supervision. Pets not allowed. January and February are busy times when various shows (hobby, craft, gems, and others) are held.

Sunflower Resort, Surprise, AZ. Country club atmosphere, gated community, mostly for seniors over 55 but has 120 sites with concrete patios for traveling RVers, well maintained, quiet. Visiting children are welcome.

Lordsburg KOA Kampground, Lordsburg, NM. Gravel, quiet, mostly shady sites.

Fort Stockton KOA Kampground, Fort Stockton, TX. Quiet, café on premises open daily for supper in season.

Alamo Fiesta RV Resort, Boerne, TX. Paved roads, quiet, well maintained, 30 miles to the Alamo in San Antonio, 67 miles to LBJ Ranch.

Oak Leaf Park Campground, Orange, TX. Our second stay at this campground. Lots of "nature" here—trees, squirrels, ducks, geese, peafowls, wild rabbits, birds, and other species, hiking trails, nature walks.

Pine Crest RV Park, Slidell, LA. Lodgepole pine–forested sites, tours and shuttle buses from campground to New Orleans (25 minutes south). Our second stay there.

Savannah South KOA Kampground, Richmond Hill, GA. Kiddie pool, dogs and cats welcome, natural landscaping with pampas grass and assorted trees, white swans float gracefully on a lake.

Lakeview KOA Kampground, Selma, NC. Adjoins a large lake, tree-shaded wide sites, quiet, cats and dogs welcome.

The Old Mill Stream Camping Manor, Lancaster, PA. This is a clean, friendly place that adjoins the Dutch Wonderland Family Amusement Park, a favorite of the Bailey family.

Round Top Campground, Gettysburg, PA. Hospitable, clean, in rural wooded setting. Offers special activities at the campground, which is only 3 miles from the Gettysburg Battlefield Visitor Center. This campground is close to the hearts of the Lathe family. Our Westminster Church of the Brethren Camping Group also enjoys spending one weekend every year there.

Sunshine Key Fun Resort and Marina, Big Pine Key, FL. (Look for the listing in the campground directory under Sunshine Key, FL.) A tropical island that offers diving, snorkeling, fishing, boating, swimming, horseshoes, tennis, and other activities as well as just relaxing. Busy time is January 1 through the end of March with another busy time in August when the crayfish/lobster fishers arrive. A favorite of the Lathes during the Christmas holiday; they make advance reservations.

Granite Hill Campground, Gettysburg, PA, and Yogi Bear's Jellystone Park, Lancaster/Quarryville, PA. These are both campgrounds that the Baileys try to include in their camping excursions each year.

Places of Interest

The places of interest listed below are the ones that attracted us as we traveled from Maryland to California and back. Visitor information is provided for each.

Willmore Lodge is a 29-room, historic pine log building now housing an interactive museum about the building of Bagnell Dam on the Osage River, which created the Lake of the Ozarks. It also houses the offices of the Lake Area Chamber of Commerce. The lodge overlooks the Lake of the Ozarks. At Osage Beach, Missouri, travel on State Route 54 to Business 54 to Lake Ozark, cross the Bagnell Dam, turn left past a white and blue sign to Willmore Lodge. Park and walk up a roadway toward the rustic Adirondack-style rambling complex of Western pine logs on a foundation of local stone and concrete that is

Willmore Lodge. Free admission.
    Lake Area Chamber of Commerce
    1000 City Parkway, Osage Beach, MO 65065
    573-964-1008
Open 9 A.M.–4:30 P.M. daily, except special holidays.

Eisenhower Center
    200 SE 4th Street, Abilene, KS 67410-2900
    785-263-4751 Fax 785-263-4218
    E-mail: library@eisenhower.nara.gov

Open daily, 9 A.M.–5 P.M., except Thanksgiving, Christmas, and New Year's Day. Beginning Memorial Day, open until 6 P.M. during the summer months.

    Admission is free to all buildings except museum: Adults $3, over 61 $2.50, under 16 free.

Buffalo Bill Historical Center
    720 Sheridan Avenue, Cody, WY 82414
    307-587-4771 Fax 307-587-5714
    E-mail: bbhc@wavecom.net   www.bbhc.org

Hours vary according to the month of year: June–September 15, 7 A.M.–8 P.M. daily. Closed Thanksgiving, Christmas, and New Year's Day. Admission: Adults $10, students 18 and over with valid ID $6, youth ages 6–17 $4, children under 6 always free. Special group rates may be available. Wheelchairs and strollers are available free at admissions desk. Eatery and gift shop on main level.

Old Faithful is a geyser in Yellowstone National Park, Wyoming. The average interval between eruptions is about 85 minutes, varying from 45 to 120 minutes. Eruptions last from 1½ to 5 minutes. Follow signs on park roads to Old Faithful.
    Yellowstone National Park
    P.O. Box 168, Yellowstone National Park, WY 82190
    307-344-7901
    www.travelyellowstone.com
    www.AmericanParkNetwork.com   www.nps.gov

Roads open May through October (weather permitting). Be aware that a road construction program is ongoing. Do not approach buffalo or bears.

Entrance admission: $20 per vehicle, which is waived if you have a $40 annual pass for Yellowstone and Grand Teton National Parks, a $65 Golden Eagle Passport to all national parks, a $10 Golden Age Passport for ages 62 and over, or a free Golden Access Passport for the blind or permanently disabled.

Grand Teton National Park, Wyoming, may be entered from the north just south of Yellowstone National Park, which we thought gave a good view as we drove south past the mountains in this range. It may also be entered from the east on State Route 26/287 or from the south on State Route 89/191.

The park is open all year. Same entrance admission information applies as for Yellowstone National Park listed above.

Grand Teton National Park
P.O. Drawer 170, Moose, WY 83012
307-739-3600

Monterey Bay Aquarium
886 Cannery Row, Monterey, CA 93940-1085
831-648-4888 Fax 831-648-4810
www.montereybayaquarium.org

Open 10 A.M.–6 P.M.; holiday and summer hours, 9:30 A.M.–6 P.M. (summer season, end of May to first of September). Parking garage, 75 cents per half-hour or less and $12.00 maximum per day.

Admission: $15.95, $12.95 over 65 or students with ID ages 13–17, $6.95 physically impaired or ages 3–12. Wheelchairs are available free at information desk.

Cannery Row shops are adjacent to the aquarium.

National Steinbeck Center
One Main Street, Salinas, CA 93901
831-796-3833 Fax 831-796-3828
www.steinbeck.org

Open 10 A.M.–5 P.M. Closed Easter, Thanksgiving, Christmas, and New Year's Day.

Admission: $7.95 adults, $6.95 seniors (over 62) and students with ID, $5.95 youth ages 13–17, $3.95 children ages 6–12, free for members and children 5 and under. Group rates available with advance reservations.

The **17-Mile Loop** is a scenic drive that begins in Pacific Grove, California, continues parallel to the Monterey Bay Country Club, and then travels along the Pacific Ocean coastline south to Pebble Beach and the Carmel Bay, where it returns to Pacific Grove by an inland route through Del Monte Forest and skirts Monterey. It can be entered by the Pacific Grove Gate, the Country Club Gate, the Highway 1 Gate, or the Carmel Gate. For information on when the road is open, call 831-625-8426 or 831-624-6669.

Admission: The toll for cars is $7.50 and includes a map of points of interest.

Roaring Camp & Big Trees Narrow-Gauge Railroad
P.O. Box G-1, Felton, CA 95018
831-335-4484 Fax 831-335-3509
E-mail: RCamp448@aol.com www.roaringcamp.com

Operating schedule varies with season. Contact above for timetable. No trains Christmas Day. Parking available for rigs as large as 40 feet long. Parking fee of $5 per car.

Directions from the north: Take Highway 1, 101, 280, or 680 south to Highway 17. Take Highway 17 to the Mt. Hermon Road exit and drive 3.5 miles to Felton. At Felton, turn left on Graham Hill Road and drive for ½ mile to Roaring Camp.

From the south: Take Highway 1 north to Highway 17 at Santa Cruz. Drive north on Highway 17 to the Mt. Hermon Road exit and drive 3.5 miles to Felton. At Felton, turn left on Graham Hill Road and drive for ½ mile to Roaring Camp.

Admission: Adult (ages 13 and older) $15; child (ages 3–12) $10; children under 3 free.

Napa Valley Conference & Visitors Bureau
  1310 Napa Town Center, Napa, CA 94559
  707-226-7459

This is a good place to obtain information on Napa and Napa Valley. When you enter the city of Napa, follow the blue-and-white signs to the public parking garage of the Tourist Information and Visitor Center.

Domaine Chandon (Winery)
  One California Drive, Highway 29
  Yountville, CA 94599
  707-944-2892 Fax 707-944-1123

San Francisco Tours from San Francisco North/Petaluma KOA Kampground

Sign up for these when you register at the San Francisco North KOA Kampground or when staying there.
  San Francisco North/Petaluma KOA Kampground
  20 Rainsville Road, Petaluma, CA 94952
  707-763-1492 800-992-2267 Fax 707-763-2668

Board at 8 A.M., return to campground at 4:30 P.M. Price: Adults $48.95; children (3–17) $29.95; children under 3, free. Family discount, 15 percent off with 2 or more children. Special rates for groups of 20 or more, senior discount (65 or over) 10 percent. These rates do not include entry fee for Golden Gate Park attractions, cable car fares, or food.

Quartzsite is a town in southwestern Arizona at the junction of State Route 95 and Interstate 10. Its population is 2,100 until January and February each year, when the population swells to over one million for its various gem, rock, mineral, RV, arts and crafts, and classic car shows, swap meets, and seasonal residents. People attend to both buy and sell. There are many campgrounds in the area as well as Bureau of Land Management lands on which to boondock. We visited in early October and all was quiet. For a schedule of shows, contact the following:

Quartzsite Chamber of Commerce
1490 Main Event Lane, P.O. Box 85, Quartzsite, AZ 85346
520-927-5600 Fax 520-927-7438
E-mail: qtzchamber@redrivernet.com
www.quartzsitechamber.com

Montezuma Castle National Monument is south of Flagstaff and north of Phoenix, Arizona, off I-17. Going north on I-17 from Phoenix, use Exit 289, go up a ramp, turn right, and drive two miles to Montezuma Castle following brown-and-white signs. (Watch for left turn shortly after turning right.) You will find a parking lot and visitor center.

Admission to the self-guided trail below the castle ruins is $2.00 per person (children under 17 free). The visitor center also includes artifacts and exhibits of vegetation and animals in the area. To do everything justice you would need an hour.

Superintendent, Montezuma Castle
P.O. Box 219, Camp Verde, AZ 86322
520-567-3322   www.nps.gov/moca

Sedona, Arizona, lays among red buttes and monoliths of Oak Creek Canyon in north-central Arizona, 120 miles north of Phoenix and 30 miles south of Flagstaff. Its elevation is 4,500 feet above sea level. From I-17, near Flagstaff, take Exit 337 to a stop sign, turn left and follow signs to Route 89A. Turn left again to Sedona on Route 89A South or Oak Creek Canyon Drive. Oak Creek Canyon Drive is a paved, two-lane road with switchbacks that descends into Sedona, 23 miles ahead. You can also enter Sedona from I-17 at Exit 330 on Route 179.

The Forest Service operates six campgrounds (total of 173 sites) in Oak Creek Canyon. Most are open from Memorial Day through Labor Day on a first-come, first-served basis. They do not have electrical hookups or shower facilities. Check your campground directory for private campgrounds in the area. One listed in our campground directory is the Rancho Sedona RV Park, 135 Bear

Wallow Lane, 888 641-4261. It offers 70 spacious sites, e-mail access, and full hookups.

Sedona-Oak Creek Canyon Chamber of Commerce
Corner of Forest Road and Route 89A, P.O. Box 478
Sedona, AZ 86339
520-282-7722 800-288-7336
www.SedonaChamber.com or www.VisitSedona.com

Campground and Truck Center Directories

Paul and I keep on board our motorhome several campground and truck center directories. They are invaluable in finding a place to stay at night, a service center should it be needed, propane, and diesel fuel. The list below includes some of the directories available in hard copy. In addition to those listed below, you may also wish to check the Internet for campgrounds and RV services on Web sites such as www.gocampingamerica.com.

AAA Campbooks
Available to members only through local AAA offices. They include campgrounds in the United States and Canada.

Anderson's Campground & RV Park Travel Directory (along the East Coast from upstate New York to the Florida Keys)
Drawer 467, Lewisburg, WV 24901
888-645-1897; 304-645-1897   Fax 304-645-1697
E-mail: camping@mountain.net
www.andersonsdirectory.com

eXitSource 2001 (formerly *Exit Authority*, will be updated annually)
eXitSource 2001 RV Directory (formerly *Travel Centers & Truck Stops*)
Interstate America
5715-B Oakbrook Parkway, Norcross, GA 30093-9943
800-683-3948
www.exitsource.com

KOA Directory Road Atlas and Kampground Guide
Kampgrounds of America, Inc.
P.O. Box 30558, Billings, MT 59114-0558
406-248-7444   Fax 406-248-7414
www.koakampgrounds.com

The RVer's Friend (lists diesel/gasoline locations and their camping services)
P.O. Box 476, Clearwater, FL 33757
800-338-6317
www.truckstops.com

Trailer Life Directory for Campgrounds, RV Parks & Services
The Trailer Life RV Campground Finder (CD-ROM)
Trailer Life Atlas
TL Enterprises Incorporated
2575 Vista Del Mar Drive, Ventura, CA 93001
800-234-3450   Fax 805-667-4454
www.tldirectory.com

Wheelers RV Resort & Campground Guide
1310 Jarvis Avenue, Elk Grove Village, IL 60007
800-323-8899; 847-981-0100   Fax 847-981-0106
E-mail: gwheelers@yahoo.com
www.wheelersguides.com

Woodall's Campground Directories (North American, Eastern, Western editions)
Woodall Publications Company
2575 Vista Del Mar, Ventura, CA 93001
877-680-6155
E-mail: woodalls@woodallsbooks.com
www.woodalls.com or www.rv.net

Yogi Bear's Jellystone Park Campground Directory
Leisure Systems, Inc.
6201 Kellogg Avenue, Cincinnati, OH 45228
513-232-6800   Fax 513-231-1191
Reservations: 800-558-2954 www.campjellystone.com

Membership Benefit Cards

Certain clubs and organizations have arranged with participating campgrounds to offer discounts to RV travelers staying on their premises. Paul and I carry membership cards for AAA, Good Sam, and KOA and stayed at Good Sam and KOA affiliated campgrounds on this trip. Further information about these cards is shown below. Other clubs and organizations also offer discounts or special membership prices at campgrounds.

AAA. Members of this organization are eligible to receive discounts at participating campgrounds when they show their AAA membership cards. In addition, AAA offers its members free maps, trip routing, and invaluable TourBook guides. Inquiries about joining may be made by checking a telephone directory for a local AAA office. Interested persons may also visit AAA's Web site or write to the following address:
AAA
1000 AAA Drive, Heathrow, FL 32746-5063
www.aaa.com

Good Sam RV Owners Club. This is the oldest and largest travel club for RVers. Annual membership dues are $25. Membership benefits include a 10 percent courtesy discount at over 1,700 participating campgrounds and RV parks in the United States and Canada,

10 percent savings on RV parts and accessories at participating facilities, 10 percent discount on LP gas, discounts on the *Trailer Life Directory for Campgrounds, RV Parks & Services,* free trip routing service, the *Highways* monthly magazine, and others. Persons may sign up at any Good Sam Park, or at the club's Web site, or by calling 800-314-3490 ext. 935 (preferred by Good Sam), or by writing to the following address:

Good Sam Club
P.O. Box 6888, Englewood, CO 80155-6888
E-mail: goodsam@goodsamclub.com
www.goodsamclub.com

KOA. The KOA Value Kard can be purchased for $10 at any KOA Kampground, at the Web site below, or by mail at the address below by sending $10 and your name and address. It is good for one year and entitles its owners to a 10 percent discount on daily registration fees at KOA Kampgrounds whether you pay by cash or credit card. It also includes a free *KOA Directory & Road Atlas* and a free issue of *Camping Life Magazine.*

KOA Value Kard
P.O. Box 31734, Dept. D, Billings, MT 59107-1734
www.koakampgrounds.com

Yogi Bear's Jellystone Park Camp-Resorts. A Club Yogi card can be bought at any participating Jellystone Camp-Resort location or by sending $20 to the address listed below with a check or money order for $20. The card is good for two years and will save you 10 percent on daily registration fees.

Leisure Systems, Inc.
6201 Kellogg Ave., Cincinnati, OH 45228

Publications

I have a friend who loves the "destination" articles in RV magazines so much that she cuts out those that she may refer to in future travels. RV magazines play important roles for RVers in other ways as well: latest laws, new products, technical articles, and other RV-related issues. Such publications are listed below:

Camperways
Camp-orama
RV Traveler
Woodall Publications Corp.
2575 Vista Del Mar, Ventura, CA 93001
877-680-6155
E-mail: info-woodalls@woodallsbooks.com
www.woodalls.com

Camping Life Magazine
Poole Publications, Inc.
P.O. Box 392, Mt. Morris, IL 61504-0392
310-537-6322

Campers Monthly
P.O. Box 260, Quakertown, PA 18951
E-mail: campersmonthly@fast.net
or WeRV2@aol.com

Family Motor Coaching
8291 Clough Pike, Cincinnati, OH 45244
513-474-3622   800-543-3622   Fax 513-474-2332
www.fmca.com

Highways
MotorHome
Trailer Life
Roads to Adventure
The RV Buyers Guide

T.L. Enterprises, Inc.
2575 Vista Del Mar Drive, Ventura, CA 93001-2575
805-667-4100   800-234-3450
E-mail: directory@tl.com
www.rv.net
www.rvsearch.com (for new and used RV listings)

Midwest Outdoors
111 Shore Drive, Burr Ridge, IL 60521-5885
630-887-7722   Fax 630-887-1958
E-mail: info@midwestoutdoors.com
www.midwestoutdoors.com

Northeast Outdoors
70 Edwin Avenue, Box 2180, Waterbury, CT 06708
(203) 755-0158

Pop UP Times
225 Mill Street NE, Vienna, VA 22180
703-938-3722   Fax 703-281-5960
E-mail: popuptimes@aol.com
www.popuptimes.com

RV Times
40th Avenue, Aldergrove, British Columbia, Canada V4W 1X2
E-mail: Sheila@rvtimes.com
www.rvtimes.com

Trailblazer
Thousand Trails, Inc.
2711 LBJ Freeway, Suite 200, Dallas, TX 75234
214-488-5021   800-328-6226
www.1000trails.com

Travelin'
860 West 6th Avenue, P.O. Box 23005, Eugene, OR 97402-0424
541-485-8533

Western RV News
64470 Sylvan Loop, Bend, OR 97701
541-318-8089   Fax 541-318-0849
E-mail: editor@westernrvnews.com
www.westernrvnews.com

Workamper News
201 Hiram Road, Heber Springs, AR 72543-8747
501-362-2637   Fax 501-362-6769
E-mail: info@workamper.com
www.workamper.com

Travelers with Special Needs

Many people with special needs find that they can travel in comfort and convenience in an RV. More than a dozen manufacturers offer RVs and conversion vans with features such as wheelchair lifts or ramps, roll-under sinks, and lower kitchen counters and cabinets.

To obtain a directory on RV accessibility for those with special needs, contact RVIA.

Recreation Vehicle Industry Association (RVIA)
P.O. Box 2999, Dept. P, Reston, VA 20195
703-620-6003   Fax 703-620-5071
www.rvia.org

Additional information on services for travelers with disabilities is available from the Handicapped Travel Club.

Handicapped Travel Club
5929 Our Way, Citrus Heights, CA 95610
916-966-7090

Driving Schools

RV driver training and schools are offered by some RV dealerships, some insurance companies (call your insurance carrier or Good Sam

VIP insurance at 800 VIP-AUTO), at many state Samborees (for Good Sam Club members), and by the following:

Life on Wheels
Gaylord Maxwell, founder
866-569-4646 (toll free)
Iowa@lifeonwheels.com
www.lifeonwheels.com
Currently offering conferences in Idaho, Pennsylvania, Kentucky.

The RV Driving School
Richard (Dick) Reed, Owner
909-984-7746 Fax 909-460-0578
rvschool@gte.net
www.rvschool.com
Currently offering year-around training in California, Oregon, and Texas. Will be opening other locations soon.

RV Trade Associations

One of the basic purposes of these associations is representing their industry to the public. They invite your inquiries.

Canadian Recreational Vehicles Association
111 Peter, Suite 527, Toronto, Ontario CANADA M5V2H1
416-971-5411
E-mail: crva@crva.ca
www.crva.ca

Recreation Vehicle Dealers Association of Canada
Suite 210, 2323 Boundary Road, Vancouver, British Columbia CANADA V5M4V8
604-718-6325 Fax 604-204-0154
www.rvda.ca

Recreation Vehicle Dealers Association (RVDA)
RV Rental Association (RVRA)
RV Aftermarket Association (RVAM)
3930 University Drive, Fairfax, VA 22030
www.rvda.org

Recreation Vehicle Industry Association (RVIA)
1896 Preston White Drive, P.O. Box 2999, Reston, VA
20195-0999
www.rvia.org

Trip Statistics

Total miles: 7,567
   Average miles per day when on the road: 261
   Most miles traveled in one day: 410
   Least miles traveled in one day: 102

Total days: 44
   Number of days not traveling in RV: 15
   Number of days boondocking as guests of friends: 5

Total spent: $4,436.90
   Average spent per day: $100.84
   Total spent for campgrounds: $987.50
   Average spent per day for campsites: $25.99
   Total spent for diesel fuel: $1,130.73
   Total gallons of fuel: 668.611
   Average cost per gallon: $1.71
   Highest price per gallon: $2.159 in CA
   Lowest price per gallon: $1.549 in LA
   Miles per gallon of fuel: 11.3

Travel Checklists

You will find a variety of checklists offered in the RV world, such as in RV magazines and from RV sales and service centers. The checklist that follows is the one Paul and I actually use. I set it up originally when we first bought our first motorhome. Over the succeeding 14 years I've refined it as I learned what we would and would not need on the road. You will want to add those items unique to your special needs, interests, and destinations, of course.

The checklists—one for Paul and one for me—include what we normally try to keep in stock in the motorhome as well as reminders of what items to take along on each excursion. Paul and I each scan our lists before heading out. They are long lists, but we have learned to scan them quickly because we know which items are already on board and which details have been taken care of. Using the checklist gives us the satisfaction of knowing that when we pull out of the driveway we have on board what we will need (or know what we have to get along the way) and that our affairs at home are handled.

Motorhome Checklist—Bernice

Kitchen and Dining Area Supplies and Equipment

- ❑ Place settings for eight—microwavable, nonbreakable dishes
- ❑ Silverware for four
- ❑ Acrylic tumblers
- ❑ Plastic knives, forks, spoons
- ❑ Plastic cereal bowls
- ❑ Paper plates
- ❑ Paper cups
- ❑ Paper napkins
- ❑ Placemats for eight
- ❑ Tablecloth and seat covers for picnic table
- ❑ Paper towels (two rolls for kitchen, one roll for windshield)
- ❑ Bottle opener

- ❏ Spatula
- ❏ Butcher knife
- ❏ Paring knife
- ❏ Serrated-edge knife
- ❏ Sieve spoon
- ❏ Measuring spoons
- ❏ Measuring cups
- ❏ Ice cream dipper
- ❏ Dish cloths (two)
- ❏ Tea towels (four)
- ❏ Hand towels, Turkish (four)
- ❏ Dishwashing liquid
- ❏ Liquid hand soap
- ❏ Laundry detergent
- ❏ Spot-and-stain remover
- ❏ Fabric softener sheets
- ❏ Quart plastic pitcher
- ❏ Electric can opener
- ❏ Windowpane cleaning liquid spray
- ❏ Waxed paper—one roll
- ❏ Plastic wrap—one roll
- ❏ Aluminum foil—one roll
- ❏ Sandwich plastic bags
- ❏ Freezer plastic bags
- ❏ Trash bags to line wastebaskets
- ❏ Clothespins (twelve)
- ❏ Clothes line
- ❏ Matches
- ❏ Candles for lighting
- ❏ Candles for birthday cakes
- ❏ Plastic water bucket, one- or two-gallon size
- ❏ Plastic wash basin

- ❑ Steel wool pads
- ❑ Plastic scrubber for removing dried-on foods from cookware
- ❑ Hot mats (four)
- ❑ Oven mitts (two)
- ❑ Fly swatter
- ❑ Tape measure
- ❑ Pen flashlight
- ❑ Wastebaskets (one for kitchen area and one for bath area)
- ❑ Floor dry mop
- ❑ Pens
- ❑ Pencil with eraser
- ❑ Eraser
- ❑ Pencil sharpener (hand-held)
- ❑ Memo pad for writing grocery lists
- ❑ Scissors
- ❑ Needle
- ❑ Thimble
- ❑ Sewing thread

Bathroom Supplies and Equipment

- ❑ Prescription medicines
- ❑ Bathroom tissue
- ❑ Chemical to deodorize holding tank
- ❑ Baking soda for toilet (alternative for chemical above)
- ❑ Toilet-bowl brush
- ❑ Facial tissues (at least three boxes—one each for bath, bedroom, passenger seat)
- ❑ Headache tablets
- ❑ Antiseptic such as Bactine
- ❑ Self-stick bandages
- ❑ Cough drops
- ❑ Upset stomach liquid or tablets

- ❏ Fever thermometer
- ❏ Bath powder
- ❏ Moleskin
- ❏ Cotton tips
- ❏ Petroleum jelly
- ❏ Lip balm
- ❏ Rubbing alcohol
- ❏ Shampoo
- ❏ Hair dryer (electric)
- ❏ Extension cord
- ❏ Insect repellent
- ❏ Toothbrush
- ❏ Toothpaste
- ❏ Dental floss
- ❏ Razor
- ❏ Hair pick
- ❏ Comb
- ❏ Spring clips for hair (four)
- ❏ Shower cap
- ❏ Deodorant
- ❏ Moisturizing cream
- ❏ Foundation liquid
- ❏ Rouge
- ❏ Makeup brushes
- ❏ Lipstick
- ❏ Hair spray
- ❏ Nail clippers
- ❏ Nail file
- ❏ Nail polish
- ❏ Nail polish remover
- ❏ Magnifying mirror
- ❏ Tweezers

- ❏ Nail scissors
- ❏ Wash cloths (four)
- ❏ Hand towels (four)
- ❏ Body towels (four)

Bedroom Supplies and Equipment

- ❏ Pillows (two)
- ❏ Sheets (two queen size)
- ❏ Thermal blanket (one queen size)
- ❏ Thermal bedspread (one queen size)
- ❏ Mattress cover (one queen size)
- ❏ Goose-down comforter (store in overhead cabinet until needed)
- ❏ Bible
- ❏ Dictionary
- ❏ Resource books for hobbies such as writing, crafts

Wardrobe Accessories and Equipment

- ❏ Extra hangers in each closet (four)
- ❏ Hats
- ❏ Lightweight boots that go over shoes
- ❏ Winter boots
- ❏ Umbrellas
- ❏ Bathrobe
- ❏ Laundry bag

Where we are going determines what other clothes we take, such as blouses, shirts, pants, skirts, coats, jackets, sweaters, shorts, vests, and shoes. I always take a raincoat. We also add everyday items such as underwear, socks, hose, shoes, pajamas, bedroom slippers, and jewelry.

Handbag Items

I use a handbag large enough to hold my camera if necessary and add the following:

- ❏ House keys
- ❏ Motorhome keys
- ❏ Car keys
- ❏ Credit cards (as few as possible—carrying only one is recommended by safety experts)
- ❏ Plastic rain cap
- ❏ Hair care instructions for hair stylists en route
- ❏ Wallet with driver's license

Living Room Supplies and Equipment

- ❏ Sofa pillows (two)
- ❏ Afghan
- ❏ Stationery
- ❏ Tablets of lined paper
- ❏ Games (playing cards and others)
- ❏ Magazines
- ❏ Home telephone directory
- ❏ Address book
- ❏ Stamps (for both first class letters and postcards)
- ❏ Broom for sweeping scatter rugs and awning outside
- ❏ Whisk broom
- ❏ Vacuum cleaner
- ❏ Journal
- ❏ Trip log
- ❏ Files from the house as relevant
- ❏ Laptop computer
- ❏ Printer that works with computer (I use an inexpensive multipurpose fax machine.)
- ❏ Paper and envelopes for printer

Driving Area Supplies and Equipment

- ❏ Sunglasses
- ❏ Calculator (to figure mileage from place to place and miles per gallon of fuel)
- ❏ Audio cassette tapes and/or CDs
- ❏ Cellular telephone
- ❏ Binoculars
- ❏ Map of each state we'll be going through
- ❏ Atlas
- ❏ Campground directory (to locate campgrounds)
- ❏ Reservation confirmations or information
- ❏ Tour books
- ❏ Magnifying glass (useful when looking at maps or atlas)
- ❏ Proof of vehicle insurance

To Do Before Leaving Home

- ❏ Turn on refrigerator a few days before leaving to be sure it works, to begin freezing ice cubes, and to load frozen foods.
- ❏ Load electric toaster if we're going on a long journey and we think we'll want toasted bread.
- ❏ Leave license plate number of RV with appropriate person.
- ❏ Leave telephone numbers and addresses of stops en route with appropriate person.
- ❏ Leave obituary file in obvious place and be sure appropriate person has a house key and knows location of important papers. (The obituary file contains our instructions in the event of death.)
- ❏ Make arrangements for mail: (1) use mail forwarding service or (2) ask appropriate person to handle mail while we are away or (3) arrange with post office to forward or hold mail.
- ❏ Get maps and tour books as needed and place in passenger seat area.

❑ Call neighbors on either side of house and perhaps across the street to let them know our departure and return dates. Also notify police of these dates.

❑ Get groceries or load RV from what we have on hand. We usually follow our normal eating patterns when on the road: (1) breakfast consists of cereal, fruit, and skim milk; (2) lunch consists of a salad, fruit, and dessert; and (3) dinner consists of a meat, two vegetables, fruit, and dessert. For snacks on the road, we choose pretzels and graham crackers. The following is our typical grocery list:

❑ Milk
❑ Bananas
❑ Salad greens
❑ Fresh grapes
❑ Cereal
❑ Peanut butter
❑ Canned fruit
❑ Canned soups
❑ Jelly
❑ Canned vegetables (small cans)
❑ Cranberry juice
❑ Sodas in individual bottles with screw caps
❑ Graham crackers
❑ Soda crackers
❑ Frozen dinners
❑ Frozen meats
❑ Ice cream
❑ Bread or rolls
❑ Margarine or butter
❑ Vegetable oil cooking spray
❑ Salt—can keep on board
❑ Sugar—can keep on board
❑ Flour
❑ Eggs
❑ Coffee for guests
❑ Individual cakes or cookies

Motorhome Checklist—Paul

Bathroom Supplies and Equipment

- ❏ Toothbrush
- ❏ Toothpaste
- ❏ Razor
- ❏ Shaving cream
- ❏ After shave lotion
- ❏ Comb
- ❏ Prescription medicines

Wardrobe Accessories and Equipment

- ❏ Bathrobe
- ❏ Coveralls
- ❏ Yellow slicker
- ❏ Baseball caps
- ❏ Short-sleeved shirts
- ❏ Long-sleeved shirts
- ❏ Jeans
- ❏ Sport trousers
- ❏ Sport shorts
- ❏ Sweaters
- ❏ Tee shirts
- ❏ Shorts
- ❏ Swim trunks
- ❏ Socks
- ❏ Handkerchiefs
- ❏ Belts
- ❏ Shoes
- ❏ Hiking boots

Driving Area Supplies and Equipment

- ❏ House keys
- ❏ Motorhome keys

- ❏ Credit and debit cards
- ❏ Senior and campground membership cards
- ❏ Registration card for motorhome
- ❏ Flashlight with spare batteries
- ❏ Sunglasses
- ❏ Swiss army knife

Living Room Area

- ❏ Files from house we want to take along
- ❏ Magazines from house we want to take along

Outside Storage Supplies and Equipment

- ❏ Folding lawn chairs (two)
- ❏ Mud rug for outside entrance steps to motorhome
- ❏ Antifreeze for water system
- ❏ Applicable tools and items such as (These may be applicable in accordance with your owner's manual.)
  - ❏ flat and Phillips head screwdrivers
  - ❏ pliers
  - ❏ wrenches
  - ❏ socket wrenches and socket set
  - ❏ a spark plug socket wrench
  - ❏ an inexpensive electric test light or voltmeter to diagnose electrical difficulties
  - ❏ quality jumper cables
  - ❏ tire-changing equipment
  - ❏ extra drive belts for the engine
  - ❏ extra coolant for chassis engine
  - ❏ extra 12-volt fuses for both coach and chassis systems
  - ❏ fuel filters appropriate for the RV
  - ❏ spare top and bottom radiator hoses
  - ❏ a few feet of extra heater hose
  - ❏ electrical wire and crimp-on terminals

- ❏ rolls of duct and electrical tape
- ❏ a few clean rags
- ❏ flares
- ❏ reflective warning signs

To Do Before Leaving Home

- ❏ Check on fuel for motorhome and tow car—fill tanks as needed
- ❏ Check on propane gas
- ❏ Obtain supply of oil for motorhome engine
- ❏ Obtain supply of oil for tow car engine
- ❏ Stop newspaper
- ❏ Get cash in $20 bills
- ❏ Pay ahead the following:
  - ❏ house and car insurance
  - ❏ vehicle fuel bill
  - ❏ gas and electric bill
  - ❏ telephone bill
  - ❏ fuel oil bill
- ❏ Lubricate chassis
- ❏ Change oil and oil filter of motorhome engine and refill, if necessary
- ❏ Change transmission oil and filter and refill, if necessary
- ❏ Check auxiliary generator to be sure it operates and check oil level and change as noted in manual
- ❏ Check front wheel bearings and brake pads
- ❏ Check radiator
- ❏ Check furnace to be sure it works properly
- ❏ Check water heater to be sure it works properly
- ❏ Check tires (spare also)
- ❏ Check all lights outside and inside to be sure they work
- ❏ Check batteries
- ❏ Take along any additional specialty tools that might be needed

❏ Take along books such as the owner's manual and literature that may be needed for maintenance or repair
❏ Check power-steering fluid
❏ Check brake fluid
❏ If going to another country, follow instructions of tour company
❏ Get proof of vehicle coverage from RV insurance provider

Itinerary

The map below shows the route we followed during our 44-day trip to California and back.

Glossary

Black water. Waste (sewage) from the toilet that is flushed into a black water holding tank, usually located beneath the main floor of the RV.

Boondocking. Camping in an RV without benefit of electricity, fresh water, and sewer utilities. Boondockers should follow the rules of courtesy and the local laws about where to camp. The term came originally from people who parked (or docked) out in the "boonies" (boondocks—remote rural areas) where there were no hookups or other luxuries such as swimming pools.

Bungee cord. An elasticized cord with a hook at each end that stretches to allow it to bind items together. Sometimes called a shock cord or just bungee.

Cabover. That part of the RV's body that extends over the cab and is used for a bedroom or storage. This RV is known as a Type C or Class C motorhome.

Campfire. A gathering around an outdoor fire for warmth, to enjoy roasting or toasting food, and for sociability.

Campground. A place to camp usually with designated sites for RVs or tents. A campground may be private or public and usually has a user fee. It also usually has a host, manager, or owner who administers the policies or rules of the campground.

Campground directory. A listing of available campgrounds with descriptions of facilities available and directions to find them.

Campground association. An organization of independent campground owners or of campground chains.

Camping club. An organization established for certain benefits related to RVing for its members. Some camping clubs are for people with a variety of RVs, some are for owners of specific brands of RVs.

Camping group. A group of RVers who get together for camping weekends or trips and social events on an informal basis, with a volunteer wagonmaster who makes reservations for campgrounds, collects deposits, and arranges social events.

Caravan tour. A group of travelers using a specific mode of transportation such as RVs to explore a selected area of the country. Commercial caravan tours may run from 10 days to 2 months and are hosted by a tour company that usually provides a wagonmaster.

Citizens Band (CB) radio. A radio that receives and sends two-way signals using a radio service licensed by the Federal Communications Commission for short-distance personal or business communications between fixed or mobile stations.

Coach. Another name for a motorhome.

Conversion vehicle. A vehicle such as a van, truck, or sport-utility vehicle, manufactured by an automaker and then modified by a company that specializes in customizing vehicles. The modifications may include sofas, windows, carpeting, paneling, seats, and accessories.

Creeper. A flatbed surface on swivel casters that allows a person to lie on it and roll around under a vehicle to look for and fix problems.

Diesel pusher. An RV with a diesel engine in the rear that pushes the coach on the road from its position in the back instead of pulling it along as does a gasoline engine located in the front of the rig.

Ding. A starburst or small break in the glass of a windshield caused by flying gravel. Also, a small dent.

Docking. Parking an RV at a place for overnight or longer.

Dropoff. A very steep descent alongside a road or highway.

Dry camping. Another name for boondocking. See above.

Dumping. To empty out, as in draining the holding tanks of an RV. Dumping is accomplished by removing the outlet safety cap and attaching a flexible hose to the outlet located on the RV holding tanks, inserting the opposite end of the flexible hose into a dumping station inlet pipe, usually located in a concrete sewer opening. *See* holding tanks.

Dump station. Usually a concrete pad with an inlet opening connected to an underground sewage system at a campground or other facility offering dumping service to RV travelers.

Fifth-wheel trailer. Similar to a travel trailer except that its construction lends itself to a bilevel floor plan. It is normally pulled by a pickup truck-style vehicle equipped with a fifth-wheel hitch fastened to the bed of the truck.

Folding camping trailer. A camping unit on wheels with collapsible walls that fold inward so that it can be towed by a car, van, or truck. Also known as a pop up.

Fresh water. Water suitable for human consumption.

Full-timing. Living in one's RV all year long. These RVers are known as full-timers.

Galley. The kitchen of an RV.

Gray water. Used water that drains from the kitchen and bathroom sinks and the shower into a holding tank, called a gray water holding tank, that is located under the main floor of the RV.

Gross combined vehicle weight (GCVW). A figure such as 19,000 pounds that is the maximum weight allowed for a fully loaded RV, including cargo, fluids, passengers, and towed vehicle.

Holding tanks. Tanks located on the RV, normally on the underside, that store fresh water, gray water, and black water. See black water and gray water.

Hooking up. Connecting the RV to a supply of electricity and water and to the sewer receptacle at a campground or other site.

KOA. Kampgrounds of America, a franchise chain of RV parks in North America that offers camping facilities to vacationers and overnighters.

Leveler disk. A silver-dollar size clear plastic disk with an air bubble inside to indicated how level a refrigerator/freezer unit is.

LP gas. *See* propane.

Missing engine. An engine that is not producing the normal amount of power.

Mobile home. A large house trailer designed to stay in one place that can only be moved by the proper towing vehicle. Usually 10 or 12 feet in width. It is not to be confused with a motorhome.

Monitor panel. A panel usually with lights and switches for checking the battery charge, space in waste tanks, LP gas, amount of fresh water in that tank, water pump operation, and other systems.

Motorhome. A self-propelled vehicle on wheels that serves as both transportation and home. It is built on a specially designed chassis and includes holding tanks and electrical, water, and sewage hookup connections. It provides complete living facilities. There are three types or classes of motorhomes: Type A or Class A looks similar to a bus, Type B or Class B is a van camper, and Type C or Class C is known as a cabover.

Nonpotable water. Water not suitable for human consumption. Usually available at dumping stations to use for rinsing out the RV's sewer hose and cleaning off the concrete apron around the inlent opening to the sewer system of the campground.

Park. Another name for a campground. *See* campground. Also, an area of land set aside by a city, state, or nation, usually in its mostly natural state, equipped with facilities for rest and recreation for the public to enjoy.

Parking. Docking; locating an RV in a site at a campground or other similar facility.

Park-model trailer. A spin-off of a recreational vehicle and a mobile home. It is a maximum of 8½ feet wide and 40 feet long, which is within the towability limits for an RV and may be parked in an RV park. Park-models have many options that movable RVs do not, such as regular appliances and furniture instead of built-ins. People who winter in one place other than their home location often opt for a park-model for their temporary living quarters.

Pop up. *See* folding camping trailer.

Potluck. A group meal to which participants bring various foods to be shared.

Propane. Also known as LP gas. A colorless, flammable liquified petroleum gas that provides fuel to the furnace, refrigerator, water heater, and stovetop range in RVs. Most campgrounds offer this product. LP gas tanks should only be filled to 80 percent of their gallonage capacity because the liquefied gas requires space to vaporize before leaving the tank.

Pull-through or pull-through site. These sites allow the driver of an RV to pull into the space, hook up, camp, and depart by simply pulling ahead onto a campground road. RV drivers appreciate them because they do not have to back into a space or site. Sometimes they are called drive-throughs.

Rear-end ratio. If your motorhome has a Chevrolet chassis with a rear end ratio of 1:4.56, it means that the drive shaft has to go around 4.56 times to turn the wheels one time. The value of knowing this is that, depending on many other factors, a vehicle with a drift shaft that has to turn a greater number of times to rotate the driving wheels one time would likely consume more fuel for distance traveled. This is not always the result because other factors are involved.

RV or recreational vehicle. A vehicle used for recreational purposes, such as camping, and usually equipped with living facilities. An RV can be a motorhome, fifth-wheel travel trailer, travel trailer, folding camping trailer, truck camper, or conversion vehicle. See individual listings.

Resort. A place where people go to relax, rest, and enjoy recreation facilities. A camping resort usually has more than the usual campground amenities, such as whirlpools, golf courses, craft rooms, planned social events, tennis courts, and others.

Rig. Another name for a recreational vehicle.

Rpms. Stands for revolutions per minute. For a motor it refers to the number of times that the motor shaft rotates per minute.

Self-contained. An RV that has facilities for cooking, sleeping, bathing, refrigerating, and heating, as well as holding tanks for the gray water (bath and dish water) and for the black water (sewage).

Slideout. A portion of an RV that can be extended from the main body in order to create larger interior space. During travel on the road it is kept within the main outside dimensions of the RV.

Snowbirds. A colloquialism for winter visitors from the northern cold climates to the southern warm regions of the United States. In Texas they are known as winter Texans.

Tag axle. An additional rear axle to carry the excess weight that the vehicle's main rear axle is not designed to support. An axle is a shaft on which a pair of wheels can rotate.

Tailgunner. A person designated to assist mainly with mechanical problems of RVs during a caravan tour.

Towable. A recreational vehicle without a motor such as a trailer, fifth wheel, or folding camping trailer (pop up) that is pulled by a motorized vehicle such as a car, van, or pickup truck.

Tow car. A vehicle such as an automobile, van, or pickup truck that either pulls or is pulled by an RV. Motorhomes often pull small cars or trucks behind them for use for short errands or sightseeing in cities.

Travel trailer. A hard-sided unit on wheels towed by an automobile, van, or truck that usually contains living quarters. It is hitched to the towing vehicle.

Truck camper. A hard-sided portable unit of living quarters designed to be mounted on the bed or chassis of a pickup truck.

Type A motorhome. *See* motorhome.
Type B motorhome. *See* motorhome.
Type C motorhome. *See* motorhome.

Unhooking. Disconnecting the electric cord from the campground outlet and storing the cord in its compartment in the RV, disconnecting the water hose from the campground faucet and storing the hose in its compartment in the RV, and disconnecting and stowing the black water hose. *See* dumping.

Unit. Another name for a recreational vehicle.

Van camper. A panel-type vehicle that includes at least two of the following conveniences: kitchen, sleeping, and toilet facilities. The RV manufacturer of this vehicle must also include 120-volt hookup and city water hookup connections, and fresh water storage. This type of RV is known as a Type B or Class B motorhome.

Wagonmaster. A leader, either hired or chosen, who guides a caravan of recreational vehicles on a trip. The wagonmaster usually makes advance reservations for campgrounds, shows, cruises, sightseeing, and group meals. A wagonmaster may also be the leader of a camping club or group who makes reservations at campgrounds, collects deposits, and arranges social events.

Winterize. Preparing your RV for winter storage in accordance with the manufacturer's instructions. It may include removing the water from the plumbing system and putting in a special antifreeze.

Index

About the Author

EXPERT RVER Bernice Beard is a veteran motorhomer whose more than 65 trips with her husband have included a 44-day caravan through Alaska and a 5-week excursion from Maryland to Arizona. She chronicled these trips in *At Your Own Pace: Traveling Your Way in Your Motorhome, Alaska at Your Own Pace: Traveling by RV Caravan, and Colorado at Your Own Pace: Traveling by Motorhome with Friends.*

A popular speaker at RV events and an often-requested guest on radio shows, Beard frequently serves as an expert resource to newspapers and magazines throughout the country. In addition, her columns and articles have appeared online, in newspapers, and in magazines, including *Holidays, BottomLine Tomorrow,* and *Family Motor Coaching.*

On the road, Beard collects information, takes photographs, and records observations in her journals. These materials and insights provide the basis for her manuscripts, such as her first book, *At Your Own Pace,* which Beard decided to write when a friend kept asking discerning questions about motorhoming.

Beard is a member of the Westminster Church of the Brethren Camping Group, the Family Motor Coach Association, the Good Sam Club, and the Holiday Rambler Recreational Vehicle Club. She also belongs to the American Association of University Women and is a charter member of the National Museum of Women in the Arts. She is listed in *Who's Who of American Women.* She and her husband continue to enjoy their motorhome, camping on weekends and taking a major trip of several weeks or months each year. New dreams and destinations always seem to call them back on the road.